A FIRST HAN
TO
BLED SLOVENIA
2017
Standard Edition

Edition number 1

Davy Sims

Copyright © 2017 by Firsthand Guides Ltd

ISBN: 9781520854168

Imprint: Independently published

www.firsthandguides.co.uk

In association with

Lake Bled News – www. LakeBledNews.com @LakeBledNews

Firsthand Guides

This edition updated 20 May 2017

DEDICATION

To my many friends in Slovenia

and to the memory of my dear friend

Rok Klančnik

who introduced me to the country.

Table of Contents

INTRODUCTION

This is an updated and amended version of the original publication produced in April 2017. Thanks to readers and friends for feedback which I have incorporated into this edition.

I first visited Bled in 1996. I stayed in Vila Bled, had dinner in Pri Planincu and met a man who was running a music festival. The Vila Bled manager showed me around. He is now Mayor of the municipality and a good friend. The man who ran the music festival is Leo Ličof the founder and artistic director of the Okarina Festival. I have lived in Bled for over a year and have many friends there. I have even attempted to learn the language. That has not been successful, but my friends find it amusing.

In due course, there will be a website to accompany the book where you can leave your comments and questions [www.firsthandguides.com]

In the meantime, feel free to follow me on Twitter (@davysims)

Davy Sims

Bled, Slovenia and Holywood, Northern Ireland

21 May 2017

"Every morning, I walk around the lake to my office. Bled is my hometown, but I admire its beauties everyday even more."

Lea Ferjan – Bled Culture Institute

Most independent travellers arrive in Bled by car or bus, which is where I begin this book. People arriving on organised holidays will have representatives to assist with their transfers and questions. In this section, I want to keep the information as practical as possible for people arriving in the town for the first time. We all carry mobile phones. Many of us are constantly connected to the internet where we can grab instant information, maps, directions and phone numbers. The aim of the book is to curate and present the information you need when you are in Bled or planning a visit; information which is practical and relevant to most visitors, but will save you the research time on the web.

The bulk of the book is written from experience. It tries to answer questions with that experience and sometimes inside knowledge. For example: when you get off the bus as you arrive for the first time in Bled, do you go right or left to get to the lake? (It doesn't matter.) Where's the best cake shop? (It matters very much!) Where can I do my laundry? (For the sake of your fellow travellers!)□

Arriving in Bled

Arriving by bus:

Most people arriving by bus are travelling from Ljubljana or from the train station at Lesce where they pick up either a local service or join the bus from Ljubljana. Others come from the Bohinj direction going towards Ljubljana. If you are arriving from Ljubljana or Lesce, Radovljica, Kranj direction, once the bus gets to the top of the hill just as you come into Bled, you will get your first sight of the town. It is more than likely that the first stop is not for you unless you are going to Hotel Krim, Union or some of the hostels and apartments nearby. You are more likely going to the Bled Bus Station (Avtobusna postaja Bled). Some first-time visitors scramble to get off here at Union stop. The drivers are used to it and will announce this is not where you want to be. Some first-time visitors ignore the driver; he knows what he's talking about, people.

When the bus pulls into the station a few minutes later, you get off at the back door. If there is a crowd, there is usually a bit of confusion. Some people wanting to board the bus will demand tickets to Ljubljana – this bus is not for Ljubljana, it is going on to Bohinj Jezero, Bohinj Zlatorog or that direction.

Slovene bus destination boards can be confusing at first. They show where the bus has come from (Ljubljana) and where it is going (Bohinj Jezero). This causes some bewilderment among new visitors which is often expressed simultaneously in many European and Asian languages. The circumstances are compounded by the timetable. The Bohinj to Ljubljana bus arrives about the same time as the Ljubljana to Bohinj bus. As you get off, other people are milling about confused about getting on.

On a hot summer's day patience is strained. I really admire most of the bus drivers who just take it in their stride, talking to the passengers, speaking three or four languages sometimes.

When people get off the bus, they usually want one of these questions answered almost immediately:

- Where is the cash machine?
- Where are the toilets?
- Where is the lake?
- Where is the coffee/beer/wine/cream cake?

So, let's answer those questions by taking a short walk from the bus to the Tourist Information Centre.

When you get off the bus it doesn't matter whether you turn left or right to go down to the lake, either will do. If you go left at the bus, take the immediate right, if you go right take the immediate left.

Coffee/beer/wine/cream cake?

Already you are spoilt for choice. Caffe Peglez'n is a small traditional place with a big terrace. It is favoured by locals as well as visitors and is one of my top three places for coffee and calm in Bled. It's on the right. Art Café is modern and attracts younger clientele including students from the two nearby colleges. A wider range of drinks is available, as are snacks and in the winter excellent hot chocolate. You can read more about them both in the Café's and Bars sections.

A few paces past the Art Café is Vinoteka Zdravljica. It is stocked with about a hundred Slovene wines. There is a dozen or so on the wine list to be bought by the glass. A personal favourite.

Where is the lake?

There it is; just past those cafés and there's the Castle up on the hill, and St. Martin's Church and the island and the view and the swans and ducks and a great big helping of the Bled experience.

Where are the toilets?

Of course, the cafés and bars have toilets. The nearest public toilets, though, are just past the Festival Hall (Festival Dvorana Bled) on the left just as you get to the horse drawn carriages. You'll need 50 cents to use the toilets. There are other public toilets (50c, too) in the main Shopping Centre.

If you only have bank notes, there is a change making machine beside the horses.

Where is the Cash Machine?

Walk on, toward the shopping area about 200 meters and you will see the Gorenjska Banka. The nearest ATM is there. Along the way, you will pass the beautiful town hall on the left. Once you have your cash, walk along a little further for the home of Bled Cream Cake, more coffee and one of the best views over the lake toward the castle.

Other questions

- Where is Tourist Information? After you leave the cash machine (bankomat) continue to walk toward the Casino. There is a sign for tourist information.
- Where can I hire a car? There are several places. You can hire a car at Hertz at Tourist Information. I always use EuropCar. The office is part of the Hotel Krim building, Ljubljanska cesta 7, 4260 Bled. Phone: +386 31 382 055
- Where can I do my laundry? The recently opened Speed Queen is near the bus station and close to most of the hostels and backpacker accommodation. It is cheap, fast, bright and clean. The whole process takes about an hour. Prešernova cesta 50, 4260 Bled. Phone +386 41 366323.
- Where's good for lunch? There is a very wide choice of places to eat. In the food and drinks section I nominate the best places I have visited. There is a more exhaustive list if you want more information.

Leaving by bus

There are two main departure points; Bled Bus Station and Union stop on the main road the Ljubljana, away from the town. As mentioned in the "Arriving by Bus" section, things can become a little confusing during the summer as people from half a dozen different countries try to work out if this is the bus they want.

Bus destination boards show (first) where the bus started its journey and the destination (second) with some other places between the two names. To add to the confusion at the station, buses going to Ljubljana and from Ljubljana arrive within minutes of each other. And finally Bled bus station serves other destinations, nearby towns and villages. It can become quite busy.

As you wait at the bus station, you are likely to see a minibus advertising rides to Ljubljana for €7, the journey taking around 40 minutes. If the driver gets enough people (8, I think) he will leave when full. The cost is only a few cents more than the bus and takes half the time. It is a good service. Consider using it. I don't know the driver, we have spoken a few times (his English is excellent) and I have seen him being very helpful to travellers who are not using his service.

Arriving by train

There are two train stations serving Bled, which is not the same as saying there are two train stations in Bled. There are not.

Bled Jezero railway station (železniška postaja) which is on the line from Jesenice is high above the north-western side of the lake. It is not well placed if you are going to the town or the hostel and hotel area. It is almost 3 kms from the town centre. The main camping ground is much closer – 10 minutes or so down a steep hill. Hotel Triglav is very close to the station. The line continues to Nova Gorica on the Italian border. Services are infrequent but it is a beautiful journey. It makes a lovely day out.

I have noticed people take the service from Ljubljana to Jesenice (not getting off at Bled-Lesce) change and then back to Jezero. That whole journey is about 3 hours. You might think it makes sense to you and your arrangements, particularly if you are going to the camp site.

Bled-Lesce railway station is 4 km from Bled. The bus stop is across the road from the train station. The service from there is good and frequent during the day. However, in the evening and on Sundays there can be long gaps between buses. The journey is about 10 minutes stopping at Bled Union and Bled bus station. It takes about an hour to walk. I imagine you could rent or buy a bicycle from the large cycle shop near the station. When all other alternatives are exhausted, you can get a taxi. Taxis from Lesce to Bled are expensive. Be prepared to pay €15 for the ten minute 4km trip. The last time I took a taxi from Lesce to Mlino the charge on the meter was a few cents short of €20 (December 2016).

Arriving by car

Parking can be difficult. If you arrive by car you will probably come via one of three directions, the Ljubljana/Jesenice highway, from Bohinj or possibly from Vintgar Gorge. On a hot busy weekend, I wish you luck. There are lots of parking places, but they fill up quickly. There is parking along cesta Svobode from around about the bus station and in front of Festival Hall. There is more parking behind Festival Hall, behind Vila Prešeren and a few other places. If you can't find somewhere easily, I suggest going out of town – not toward Mlino, you have no chance there, but toward Ljubljana. The two main petrol stations are on Ljubljanska cesta on the road towards the highway. There is a useful map here [www.bled.si/en/how-to-get-here].

If you plan to visit Mlino, there is a large abandoned building just past Vila Bled. The space around it is used by tour coaches for parking. You might find some room there. The walk all the way back to the town centre is about 25 minutes. But what a walk!

Arriving by motorbike
You will see signs outside many of the bars and restaurants here in the Gorenjska region welcoming bikers. Touring bikers are often seen on the winding mountain roads. Harley Davidson clubs meet in Bled during the summer. The information for bikers is the same as everyone else, but you might want to prioritise places were bikers are particularly welcome. You have a

14

better chance of meeting likeminded people and get advice and suggestions for your visit.

You are here!

Now you have arrived and dealt with personal needs like laundry, cash, coffee, and cake, you can start exploring.

Where to get information when you arrive in Bled - Tourist Information

The Tourist Information Centre is in the main shopping area beside the Casino. The staff are very friendly and knowledgeable. They will have information about what is going on in Bled and the surrounding area. They will can usually help you with other questions about Slovenia. You can also hire a bike or car (Hertz).

Turistično društvo Bled, cesta Svobode 10 4260 Bled. Phone: +386 (0)4 5741 122

Opening Times: Mon - Sat: 8:00 am - 7:00 pm Sun: 10:00 am - 4:00 pm

If you are a serious walker, hiker, cyclist, climber or adventure tourist/traveller and plan to explore the Triglav National Park, the first stop should be

Infocenter Triglavska roža Bled Ljubljanska cesta 27, SI - 4260 Bled. Phone: +386 (0)4 5780 205

E-mails:

- Bled: info@dzt.bled.si,
- Slovenian Alps: info@slovenian-alps.com,
- Triglav National Park: info.trb@tnp.gov.si

Opening times: Spring and Summer, every day from 8.00 am to 6.00 pm. Rest of the year every day from 8.00 am to 4.00 pm.

There is a permanent exhibition about the Triglav National Park, a book and souvenir shop, and a nice little café.

Shopping for survival and recreation

There are two reasons to shop; because you need something and because you want something. Sometimes you just want to shop. Food and day to day shopping are straight forward. There are several supermarket chains in Slovenia; Mercator, Tuš, Spar, Hoffer and Lidl among them.

Shopping for survival and groceries

There are at least 6 Mercator shops in Bled. The biggest is Kajuhova cesta 1. It re-opened refurbished in March 2017 and is great for a big family shop. Another large one is on Ljubljanska cesta near to Gostilna Union. There is a mid-sized Mercator in the main shopping centre. Three smaller Mercators can be found at Campsite at Zaka, Mlino and Prešernova cesta near most of the hostels. The opening times of the smaller shops depend on the season and the Mercator at the campsite is closed in the winter. As a rough guide, they are open by 8:00 am and closed by 6:00 pm Monday to Friday. Weekend opening hours are more limited. In the winter, for example Mlino is closed on Sundays. Opening times are displayed at the entrance.

There was a Tuš in Bled, but now the nearest is in Lesce where you will also find Spar (Alpska cesta 34). Lidl and Hofer is out of town at Hraška cesta 22.

Important Tip: When you are buying loose fruit and vegetables, after bagging what you want WEIGH THEM and get a PRICE STICKER before going to the checkout desk. That info was so important I used capitals.

Heavy duty shopping

If you are visiting Bled for a few days, you won't need to know about the Trgovski Centre just outside Lesce at 51

Rožna Dolina where you will find an even bigger Mercator and Merkur. The Merkur is for significant household items. If you are moving to Bled or spending a long period there, this is where you will find pots and pans, duvets, DIY tools, bedside lamps and all the other essentials to set up a home. You will need a car to get there and back if you are doing a big shop.

Shopping for fun

Huberto Široka is probably the best-known jeweller in Bled. His shop at cesta Svobode 19 Bled. Phone: +386 (0)40 22 68 05 [www.hubertos.net], is just opposite the Grand Hotel Toplice.

Huberto was born in Zagreb in 1960 spending his childhood in Paris and Bled. He started his career as a goldsmith at the age of 24. In 1990, he officially became an International Master of Fine Arts and decided to become an independent culture worker. He has exhibited throughout Slovenia and abroad.

Much of his work is inspired by Bled and the surrounding area. He tells me. "In my work, there is a lot of the history of Bled, which I'm trying to maintain and add to the inspiration of the present. Years ago, I made one of the most beautiful archaeological finds "Peacock – bird of Eden". It is a symbol of Bled and brings people laughter and happiness. Happiness comes when people laugh.

"The source of my inspiration is the path around the lake and in all seasons - summer, autumn, winter, spring - when the rain falling or snow, when the sun is shining, all times of the day or night, it always brought me calmness."

There are two markets you should know about. The Triglav market is held every third Saturday in the month at the Information Centre, Triglavska roža Bled. It is open between 10:00 am and 12:00 noon. The Arts and Crafts Fair on cesta Svobode near the Festival Hall is open every Friday, Saturday and Sunday from 10:00 am to 7:00 pm from Spring to Autumn. It features work by Slovenian crafts people and artists who staff the stalls themselves and are very happy to discuss what's on offer.

Occasional food markets pop up during the summer. The Italian market was a real treat for the eye and the taste buds. Some farms are open to visitors during the year. One to visit is homestead pr'Dornk, in Mlino, 200 meters from the lake (follow the sign to Selo). You might have to book ahead depending on the time of the year. There is more information on their website [dornk-bled.com/home].

In the centre of the town there are two principle shopping areas. One is largely tourist shopping in the shadow of the Park Hotel, the other is the Shopping Centre opposite which you can't miss – even if you wanted to.

Trgovski Centre (or just, The Shopping Centre)

The shopping centre is known locally as the Gadafi Centre. Slovenes like a good story and the story or explanation as to why such an extraordinary structure is found on the shore of one of the prettiest places in the world is that it was originally intended for Libya. No-one has yet been able to explain to me why or how it was built in Bled rather than Tripoli. However, researching for this book I have found that the website for the shopping centre [www.shopping.si] titles its homepage "Domov Gadafi" and "Gadafi" is a search term on the website. Perhaps it is more than a nickname.

There are sixty outlets on four floors set around a main piazza where you can sit out in the sun – shaded by big umbrellas – and order coffee, snacks and drinks. Which café will serve you will depend on where you sit. There are other bars, cafés and restaurants around the centre and the views are much better looking out than looking in. You will also find clothes shops, sports shops, a tiny wine shop stocked with Slovene wines. It is an open sunny and relaxed spot where you can sip drinks and top up your tan, or find cooler corners under shade.

Often in the summer, it becomes one of the concert venues, especially for the Golden Microphone competition. More about that and other music events elsewhere in this book.

Even if you are in Bled for a short time, have a quick look around. You might be able to buy everything you need in one visit, then go on to enjoy what you came to Bled to do.

Money

Slovenia is in the Euro-zone. As a country, it has a reputation for being comparatively inexpensive. Bled and Ljubljana are more expensive than other parts of Slovenia, but still ... the costs are pretty good. Compare: €1 for a dolga kava (long black coffee) in Bled €2.50 in Dublin.

You will need to carry change. I really don't know why, but the shops are always looking for exact change. This is not unique to Bled. Finding the right coins is almost a national sport. This is not helped by the ATMs that insist on spitting out €50 notes which are often held in contempt in some shops if you are making a small purchase.

The two most easily found banks are Gorenjska Banka, cesta Svobode 15 (Monday - Friday: 8:00 to 11:30 and 14:00 to 17:00 Saturday: Closed) and SKB Banka in the shopping centre (Hours: Mon-Fri 8:30 to 12:00 and 14:00 to 17:00, Saturdays closed). But don't take your €50 note to the bank teller and ask for it to be changed - there will be a charge.

PART 2 – BEST TIMES TO VISIT

From the excitement at the height of the summer when music fills the air around the lake, to the cold winters where, if you are lucky, you can skate on the frozen surface as they did 2011 and 2016, there is always something to bring you back to Bled.

Spring (March, April, May)

Once the Christmas tree is taken down and the Christmas market packs up for another year, the town becomes very quiet. There are still some winter activities – the ice-rink, Straža, skiing and the occasional event in Pokljuka – but the town accepts that it is time for a communal winter snooze.

The sound of a big brass band heralds the beginning of spring and the Easter celebrations bring the town – and the tourists – back to life. The traditionally liveried Godba Gorje brass band play at every significant occasion in Bled and the nearby villages. The Municipality of Gorje is about 5 km from Bled, but many of the musicians are from the town. It has represented Bled and Slovenia around the world over the decades. They look impressive and the sound they make is the sound of Gorenjska. The Easter activities and the season have begun.

It is no exaggeration to say that Bled is a sunny place. The sun shines year-round and while there are sometimes torrential showers, and rain lasting for days on end even in the summer, you are more likely to experience a sunny day any time of the year. Spring brings cool days and evenings. You might experience a night time thunder storm from spring through summer.

Spring is overall a quiet time. Inter-railing students arrive from mid-May, but mostly it is quiet, sunny and fresh.

Summer (June, July, August)

It can be hot. During this period friends who have lived a long time in Bled report temperatures of up to 40C. I have enjoyed 35C for more than 10 consecutive days in July and August. There is no guarantee there won't be rain, but it is unlikely.

Events start to build. They climax in the music and sporting festivals which dominate the summer. The restaurants and bars are at their best, the days are long and the nights are hot. And people are extremely well behaved. There is little or no public drunkenness, you will feel (and are) safe. The buses are full, the roads are busy and at times the town gets choked.

I like to disappear on Saturday and Sunday afternoons. It is easy to find quiet walks away from the buzz of the holiday centre. There is no Bled bypass (although planning permission was granted in March 2017), so the road through the town is also the route to other tourist centres like Lake Bohinj or Triglav National Park.

Autumn (September, October, November)

The colours around the lake change – it is spectacular. From about mid-August you can feel a change. As the church bells peal around Bled and other towns and villages on 15 August for the feast of the Assumption, you may feel a change in temperature. There is a pleasant breeze and the evenings are cooler. And there are more photographers around the lake capturing the new colours emerging from the green hillsides. By the end of November some of the mountain peaks begin to turn white.

There are still activities around the town, but fewer and some places begin to close. There are not as many tourists and significantly fewer day trippers. Even though the tour buses still come and expel their exhausts into the clean Alpine air, this is my favourite time of the year.

Winter (December January February)

December arrives as does the Christmas market. Since 2015, Bled has set up a market near the shore of the lake with entertainment every evening and highlights during the month. With the Christmas lights and the music, there are fires to keep you warm and benches and trellis tables to eat and drink at. Blankets are provided.

There is a party on New Year's Eve when temperatures are -10C or lower. Fireworks mark the end of the old year and the beginning of the new.

PART 3 – EVENTS THROUGHOUT THE YEAR

Music

People come to Bled all year round, but the busiest time is, unsurprisingly, the summer. It is also the time when the town is most active. Sports events and music dominate, but there are many other cultural occasions, too.

Three music highlights combine around July and August and together provide the most exciting and exhilarating part of the year. They are Festival Bled, Okarina Festival and Bled Days and Bled Nights. If you are very lucky and can spend a lengthy period in Bled, you will remember this time for years to come.

Festival Bled is a classical music event featuring extraordinarily talented young musicians from around the world, most of whom are studying in the region. There is often a jazz component and there will be in 2017. The festival, was founded and is led by internationally known violinist and native of Bled, Jernej Brence. It is held in the first two weeks of July. The young musicians participate in masterclasses with leading virtuosos and famous music teachers – usually but not always Slovenians. During that week and throughout the second week there are concerts from the masterclass tutors and other established classical musicians. In 2017, the jazz masterclass line-up includes classical and jazz singer Jadranka Juras, guitarist Jani Moder and jazz and rock drummer Janez Gabrič who plays with the legendary Slovenian band, Laibach. The classical masterclass includes violinist Michael Frischenschlager, Finnish violinist Päivyt Meller, Sandor Javorkai from Hungary, Poland's Piotr Jasiurkowski Poland and cellist Karmen Pečar.

The concerts are not just for serious music aficionados. The music is very accessible and often the concerts are by ensembles and musicians playing in a unique and entertaining way. If nothing else, should you be in Bled and the jazz music concert with the young musicians is on at the same time, do not miss it.

For up-to-date information on the Festival including concerts and venues. visit the website [www.festivalbled.com/]. For news of events and people participating search "Festival Bled" on Facebook.

Swinging Bled dance festival from 27 to 30 July will for the third year, bring memories and the style of the 1920s, 1930s and 1940s. Over three days young, enthusiastic and professional dancers revive the Slovenian swing scene. To participate as a dancer, you will need to register in advance at the event website [swingingbled.com/register].

Okarina Festival begins just as Festival Bled ends. Sometimes they overlap a little. The two festivals are celebrations of music and share some of the same venues – Festival Hall and Bled Castle – but they are very different. For Okarina, a stage is built on the Promenade giving the audience incredible views of the musicians and mountains in the background as the sun sets. Musicians from around the world come to play in this unique setting. The 27th Okarina Festival will be held at from July 27 to August 6 2017, each evening at 8:30 pm at both Bled Castle and Promenade.

For news of the line-up and details of venues plus profiles of the artists, visit the festival website [http://www.festival-okarina.si/en].

Golden Microphone is another international festival of talented singers. While it is open to all ages, it predominately features children and young people. In 2017. it will be held between 18 and 23 July. [bled-goldenmic.si/en/]

Accordion Festival began in 2013. In early summer accordionists, accordion clubs, professional musicians, learners, amateurs and lovers of the sound descend on Bled and spend at least a day playing all over the town.

It is one of the most joyful events of the year. The climax is when all the musicians line the lake shore in Spa Park to play one song together, Slavko Avsenik – "Otocek sredi jezera" (Island in the middle of the lake). They all play in the same key (well, most of them), but the speed seems to be entirely at the discretion of each group. It is a wonderful experience. In 2017, it will be held on 21 May. If you have missed it already you should keep an eye out for next year. It's worth a trip to see. Search YouTube for "Main Accordion Performance" and "400 Accordions" to see how they performed in 2014 and 2015.

Folk Music Hit Parade will be held in the Sport Hall, the biggest venue in the town. Around 2,000 people will be there to enjoy Oberkrainer bands – traditional and folk music of the Alps. Slovenia, Austria, Bavaria, Switzerland, are usually all represented on stage and in the audience.

In 2017, it will be held on 18 November at 8:00 pm. It is an energetic, exciting celebration of a music style that developed in this area and based on the tradition of Alpine folk music, modernised and electrified. Book tickets in advance through Bled Tourism's website www.bled.si/en/

Guest DJs and Clubs throughout the summer play dance music inside and out. One of the most popular places in Kult Klub, Ljubljanska cesta 4. There are updates on their Facebook page [www.facebook.com/KultBled].

For more information about events in Bled, the tourist board have a very good website at [www.bled.si/en].

Bled – Insider Knowledge:

"This is my first tip. During Festival Bled, take a nice walk to Grand Hotel Toplice for a concert of young musicians and then, if you are in the mood, walk to Villa Prešeren for a drink on terrace by the lake.

"Or, for early morning, from Jarše, on the way to village Ribno, along the paths in the fields, walking, running or cycling to Dobra gora - a little hill next to Straža - and try yoga or just sit on a bench and admire the landscape."

Mojca Polajnar Peternelj

Sports Events

In 2016, Bled was winner in the Sports Destination category at the World Tourism Awards in London. Summer is the main sports season in the town, but some winter and ice sports also feature, not the least being ice hockey and skiing. Son of Bled, Anze Kopitar, plays for LA Kings hockey team. He is a local hero and many young players see him as a role model. Naturally, most of the sport goes on in or around the lake and in the Sports Hall (Športna dvorana).

Ice Hockey U18 World Championship, the Sports Hall, 7 - 13 April 2017, and 15 - 21 April 2017.

Rowing – Bled has been a sports and health destination for over 100 years. Rowing championships are held, and there is a fantastic rowing centre on the lake (Županičeva cesta 9, Phone: +386 (0)4 5767 230 email: info@vesl-klub-bled.si [www.en.vesl-klub-bled.si/]).

There are plenty of opportunities for leisurely rowing on the lake, but if you take the sport more seriously here are a few key dates.

- The municipality has hosted four world championships. In 2017, it will be hosting the. World Rowing Masters Regatta and in 2018 the European Masters Swimming Championship for veterans.
- 58th First-May rowing regatta on Lake Bled, 22 and 23 April 2017
- The June rowing event The International Rowing Regatta, (9 – 11 June) has been held at Lake Bled for over 60 years.
- World Rowing Masters Regatta 2017 Lake Bled, Velika Zaka, 6 – 10 September 2017
- 27th National Rowing Championship Lake Bled, Velika Zaka, 24 September 2017, 10:00 - 19:00.

Check the rowing centre and bled.si websites for up to date information.

In the winter Bled is the centre for biathlons.

Chess has been a feature of the sports calendar since 1930. The Bled Chess Festival is usually held in March at the Toplice Hotel (cesta Svobode 12, 4260 Bled. Phone: +386 4 579 16 00. To participate contact the organisers. The official websites are www.caissa.si, www.sahklub-ljubljana.com)

Bled Triathlon is held at the Rowing Centre, Mala Zaka. In 2017, it will be on 24 June.

Cycling is a competitive sport, it is also the most convenient way to get around Bled. Cycle hire is widely available. However, people staying at least two months could buy a bike in Lesce and sell it back when they move on (just a suggestion).

The Bled Bike Festival is the leading bike festival in Slovenia and takes place in Bled from 25th to 27th of August 2017. [www.bledbikefestival.com is the official website]

Organised running events are held all through the summer with the annual Business Run held in May. The 10k Night Run will be on 8 July 2017. The largest run of the year is around Lake Bled and is open to registered competitors. Keep up with developments and register at the website [www.nocna10ka.net/eng]

A more social and less competitive event is Bollé Original Lake Bled Run held in August.

Walking. Is it a sport? Is it a therapy? Is it a cultural or community event? Arnold Rikli brought health tourism to Bled over a hundred years ago, and now once a year an early morning walk is held in his honour. The 19th Rikli's Walk to Straža hill will be at 7:00 am on 2 July 2017 meeting in front of Hotel Golf.

Walking and hiking are popular and a serious business in Bled and in the whole region. If you are planning a walking holiday contact the Infocenter Triglavska roža Bled Ljubljanska cesta 27, Phone: +386 (0)4 5780 205

Fishing goes on all year round. You will need to purchase a licence. Find out the details of licence fees and regulations for the lake and for the nearby Sava Bohinjka and Radovna rivers at Fauna Slovenia Fly Fishing, cesta Svobode 12, Phone: 00386 41 633 147. [www.faunabled.com]). If you are already in town you will find the shop opposite the bus station.

There are more detailed rules and regulations at this website: [https://www.ribiska-druzina-bled.si/price-list/?lang=en]

Any other sports?
Well, you could try: Alpine and sport climbing, Ballooning, Bellyak, Geocaching, Golf, Hydrospeed, Sky Diving, Horseback riding, Caving, Cycling, Kayaking, Mini golf, Motorcycling, Beach volley, Paintball and Airsoft, Summer tobogganing, Diving, Hiking, Rafting, Canyoning, Walks, Tennis and squash, Tubing, Boating, Zipline, Alpine Skiing & Snowboarding, Biathlon, Ice climbing, Sledding, Cross-country skiing, Ski Touring, Snowshoeing which are all suggestions from the Bled Tourism website.

Four adventure shops and agents in Bled:

- Rafting Bled, Grajska cesta 4, 4260 Bled. Phone: +386 51 399 164 [tinaraft.si],
- 3glav Adventures, Ljubljanska cesta 1, 4260 Bled. Phone: +386 41 683 184 [3glav.com]
- Mamut Slovenia, cesta Svobode 4a, 4260 Bled. Phone: +386 40 121 900
- LIFE Events and Ribit gift shop, Grajska cesta 10, 4260 Bled Phone: +386 4 20 14 875 info@lifeevents.si

Bled – Insider Knowledge:

"I am not the cyclist I once was, but I still like to get away from the centre of Bled at times. Tourists are very welcome, but it's good to avoid them sometimes.

I cycle out from the centre on Ljubljanska cesta. Turn right and follow the signs to Koritno - about 5km. Sometimes I turn here and follow the sign back to Selo. Other times I will cycle on to Bodešče and cross the Sava before returning.

There are lots of paths and roads to explore here and you are only a few kilometres from Bled. I always bring a phone, water and something to eat. Maybe spend the whole day exploring. In the summer - drink plenty of water. It can get very hot and there is not a lot of shade in places.

Joško

Bled Castle

Although Bled Castle organises events throughout the year independent of the town's tourism events, it is very much part of the community. Open every day for tours and visits, it also has an outstanding restaurant and spectacular views of the lake and surrounding area.

One of the main attractions is historical re-enactments. As you can imagine, children love swordfights between medieval knights and then they hold the swords themselves and mock fight with the same knights. A training camp is set up in the spring to exhibit archery, swordsmanship and other knights' skills. But inside the ancient building houses a state of the art audio visual tour and history of the area and the castle.

Historically this was a defensive and administrative castle rather than the home of kings and princesses and as you look over the walls you can understand why this was such a strategically important place. Two significant dates in the founding of Bled and the castle are 1004 (a date you will often see around Bled) and 1011. In 1004 Emperor Henry ll of Germany gave his estate at Bled to Bishop Albuin of Brixen. Brixen today is in the Province of Bolzano in Italy's South Tyrol, a distance of over 260 kms, a 4-hour car journey. The second key date is 1011 when building began. It was then just the Romanesque tower (which is still there) behind high walls. Ironically while over the centuries millions of people have come to visit Bled and the castle, the 11th and 12th century Bishops of Brixen did not.

This area was once The March (or Margraviate) of Carniola a south-eastern state of the Holy Roman Empire in the High Middle Ages, the predecessor of the Duchy of Carniola. The castle at that time would have been a possession of the Holy Roman Emperor. The Emperors' interests in the area – defensive, tax collection, development of the region – would have been carried out by the appointees and agents who lived and ruled from the castle.

This, the oldest castle in Slovenia is one of the country's principal tourist attractions, along with Postojna Cave, Lipica Stud Farm, and Ljubljana and its Castle. Throughout the middle ages (and continuing up to the present day) additional buildings, towers and modifications were made to the castle. The building is organised around two court yards. At one time the castle servants would have lived in the outer area.

The gothic castle chapel on the upper courtyard was built in the 16th century, and was renovated in the baroque style around 1700. The castle also houses a printing shop, wine cellar, forge, Knights' Hall, museum and café. The castle restaurant is said to be one of the best in Slovenia. You can drop in to eat during the day, but call to reserve in the evening.

Because of the romantic setting, the castle – and really, all Bled – has become a favoured place for weddings. You never know, you might be inspired.

From the castle walls, you can post your photos directly to social media using the free wifi. Tag them #LakeBled or #BledCastle and follow @BledCastle on Twitter.

The castle website is [www.blejski-grad.si/en]

Bled Castle Events

The culture and entertainment of the middle ages are celebrated all summer long by the Knight Gašper Lambergar Theatre Group. Dressed in costume, they demonstrate skills like medieval dances, knight duels, fire craft, and fire eating performances. The "Count and Countess of the Castle" attend official visits, weddings and other events.

Exhibitions are held throughout the year in the upper gallery of the Printing Room. The paintings and photographs are usually by local and Slovene artists.

Lectures and musical events are held throughout the year, and often the music events are for children and families.

Easter is celebrated with Easter egg hunts and games for children. There is a strong focus on events for children including some of the medieval themed events where children can become apprentice knights.

Other annual events include:

- Medieval days – usually held in June.
- Summer museum night.
- Baroque and medieval performances by the Cultural Society of Knight Gašper Lambergar held in the Upper Terrace from June to September, every Tuesday and Thursday, 5.00pm.
- The castle plays host to some Festival Bled concerts in Knight's Hall and Okarina Festival in the Upper Terrace.
- As Hallowe'en approaches the Medieval Camp sets up for a week in the parking area below the castle.
- The Halloween event for children is a specular afternoon and evening of games, dance, costume and face painting and a few scary, creepy things too.
- St. Martin's wine tasting. St Martin's Day is the day that the grape juice turns to wine in Slovenia and the day is celebrated on the Upper Terrace with traditional music, dance and storytelling.
- Christmas and New Year events are also held at the castle.

For up to date information about events at Bled Castle check their website [http://www.blejski-grad.si/en] and Bled Tourism website [www.dled.si/en]

Getting to and from Bled Castle

In the 11th and 12th century, castles were not built for easy access, quite the opposite they were built for protection. Consequently, in modern times castles are difficult to reach. Bled Castle is high above the town and the lake and if you are travelling by road the main entrance is at the top of Grajska cesta.

If you are driving from the town, take Prešernova cesta (traffic lights at the Pension Union/Union Bar) to where it meets Grajska cesta, the road to the carpark just outside the castle walls.

The travel agency Bled Tours, Ljubljanska 7, organises daily trips to the Castle. Details at their shop.

Walking (I have even seen people jogging) from the town, there are some paths up the side of the hill. The easiest to access is from St. Martin's church.

The final path once you go over the draw bridge, is itself very steep. Inside there are lots of steps. The stunning views reward the effort, whether the day is bright and sunny or cloudy and moody. A photograph does not quite encapsulate the views across Gorenjska.

Bled Insider Knowledge:

Bled Castle is a well-known cultural monument which attracts crowds of visitors from all over the world. However, hidden in the forest of the Višče Hill under the castle is a monument dedicated to Lord Adolf Muhr, a merchant from Vienna who owned Bled Castle between the years 1882 and 1919.

"Muhr built the villas Rog and Zlatorog on the shore of Lake Bled. Certainly, each are a dream location for everyone. Beside the monument, there is a bank where you can sit down and enjoy the view of the crystal clear lake below, or just listen to the silence, or breathe in the fresh alpine air.

Lea Ferjan

The whole point of Firsthand Guides is to give you personal recommendations of places the writer has been. The suggestions are my personal choices. They are places I, my family and my friends like. I have not been to every pub, café and restaurant in Bled. I have been to most. I pay my own way and do not receive any inducements to write about these places.

5 Best places for coffee

My Favourites:

I cannot settle for one; I have three favourites. They are each different, unique in their style. They do great coffee and have a few snacks. The staff are helpful and friendly and their menu extends beyond just coffee if you want to dally a little longer.

Apropos

Ljubljanska cesta 4, Bled 4260. Phone: +386 4 574 40 44

There are six or seven places for coffee, drinks or food in the shopping centre. Music themed Apropos has the style and the tasteful background music as well as excellent coffee.

Caffe Peglez'n

cesta Svobode 8a, 4260 Bled, Slovenia

This is a very stylish little café. There are views of the lake and castle, there is natural shade from overhanging trees. Favoured by locals as well as visitors. Good coffee, some snacks. Great first thing in the morning.

Caffe Belvedere

Svobode 18, 4260 Bled, Slovenia Phone: +386 (0)4 575 37 21

This is an historic building designed by Jože Plečnik who was also responsible for much of classic Ljubljana and parts of Kranj. The elegant building on stone stilts in the grounds on Vila Bled was known as Tito's Tea Room. It has outstanding views of the lake and is so close to the island you feel like you could reach out and touch it. Only open in the summer months.

Other recommendations

Art Café

cesta Svobode 7a, 4260 Bled, Slovenia Phone: +386 4 576 71 79

It is popular with students from the business school and the hospitality college nearby and with younger tourists. People mostly sit outside. It is open from about 8:00 am but gets lively in the evening when it turns into a bar and stays open until the small hours.

Jasmin Tea Room

cesta Svobode 10, 4260 Bled, Slovenia Phone: +386 4 574 38 27

Hidden away from the hustle and bustle of a busy shopping area, this small interesting tea room is beside the Tourist Information office. It rarely gets too busy and you can sit in the largish restaurant area or on the small terrace and take tea. One of the few places in Bled that serves really good tea as well as fruit flavoured infusions.

5 Best pubs

As in most of continental Europe, there is less of a pub culture than you find in the UK, the States or Australia and New Zealand. Bars here are usually restaurants and cafés as well. Some places change their character as the day progresses from coffee shop in the morning to loud party pub in the evening.

My Favourite:

With the usual caveat, these are my favourites and reflect my taste. There are two at the top of the list.

The George Best Back Bar

Grajska cesta 21a, 4260 Bled, Slovenia

This is an off the beaten track sports bar favoured by backpackers and adventure holiday makers during the summer. In the winter when the tourists are gone it is an after-work pub for locals. It is named after the Manchester United and Northern Ireland footballer George Best and consequently attracts supporters of both of those teams. It is a good basic bar and any time I have been (pretty often, to be honest) there has been a 1970s rock soundtrack in the background.

Pri Planincu

Grajska cesta 8, 4260 4260 Bled, Slovenia Phone: +386 4 574 16 13

Small bar, part of a traditional restaurant with a pizzeria upstairs. This is the first bar I ever visited in Bled in 1996 and it is still the place I go to first. While the Belvedere Pavilion is historic for being the tea room of kings and presidents, Planincu is historic for being the pub of ordinary working people in Bled. Because, if you remove tourism from this town, it is essentially a rural farming community. Pri Planincu is part of the community, although, it attracts tourists in droves. An owner must be a motorbike fanatic. The walls and ceiling are decorated with vehicle number plates. I have spotted a motorbike in the rafters of the pizzeria. As mentioned earlier, many bars and restaurants in the region especially welcome bikers. This is one.

Other Recommendations

The Cult Club

Ljubljanska cesta 4, B4260 Bled, Slovenia

In the shopping centre building but with a door onto the main road, this is a bar for younger people which in the evening becomes a music venue. It is comfortable and plays a loud (but not too loud) music soundtrack during the day. On a hot day, it is cool and shaded inside.

Pub Bled

cesta Svobode 19a, 4260 Bled, Slovenia Phone: +386 4 574 26 22

Adjacent to the shopping centre this is a quiet and dark during the day often turning into a party pub in the evening.

Devil Bar

cesta Svobode 15, 4260 4260 Bled, Slovenia

A large terrace outside and a large interesting interior. Once again, a place to escape on a hot afternoon. An enthusiastically loud party pub at night at the height of the summer.

Best pizza

Pizza is very popular in Slovenia, and not just among tourists. The pizza restaurants I have been to in Bled and Ljubljana are of a very high standard. I expect these 5 suggestions are not the only places to get pizza in Bled. Menus are all quite extensive and most pizza restaurants have dozens of toppings to choose from.

Pri Planincu Pizza

Grajska cesta 8, 4260 4260 Bled, Slovenia Phone: +386 4 574 16 13

You might have already noted I have nominated Pri Planincu as my favourite bar. It's also on the list for favourite restaurants for Slovene food. It happens to be one of my favourite places overall. Even travel writers have favourite places. The restaurant is upstairs very traditionally Alpine with wood panelling and wooden decorations. There are dozens of toppings, beer at a reasonable price and great service. There is a small terrace open in the good weather. This is a family friendly place where English, German and Italian are spoken or understood.

Picerija Briksen

Ljubljanska cesta 5, 4260 Bled, Slovenia

You will find Briksen at the Sports Hall. I have only ever been inside to order and to pay; almost everyone eats outside. You will find a good selection of toppings. Look out for a special celebration pizza for the Slovenia hockey team's performance at Sochi winter Olympics. In addition to pizza there are burgers, sandwiches.

Pizzeria Rustika

Riklijeva cesta 13, 4260 Bled, Slovenia

Rustika has a very good reputation and is often said to make the best pizza in Bled. I don't agree, I'm not sure there is a "best". Here the cooking is very good, the pizzas first class. You will not be disappointed. The restaurant is particularly cosy in the colder days of autumn and winter. It has a delivery service.

Pizzeria Gallus

Ljubljanska cesta 4, Bled 4260, Slovenia

In the Shopping Centre, pizza Gallus has a view from above the piazza. I have ever been to Gallus. There are mixed reviews.

Pizzeria Rikli

cesta Svobode 15, 4260 Bled.

This is part of the Park Hotel. I have never been, but I wonder what on earth Arnold Rikli would think of a pizzeria named after him.

Special mentions

Places that don't fit conveniently into any list or are in a league of their own – personal recommendations.

Slaščičarna Šmon

Grajska cesta 3, 4260 Bled, Slovenia Phone: +386 4 574 16 16

This cake shop fits into a category of its own, "best pastry on the planet", and probably rates very high in any league of cafés and restaurants. The cakes are superb. The restaurant is famous and it deserves the reputation. If you go nowhere else in Bled, walk up hill from the bus station and take coffee and cake here. There is another smaller more modern Slaščičarna Šmon near Union bus stop, but this is the original and best.

Slaščičarna Šmon has been part of the culture of Bled for over 100 years. At the climax of Bled Nights when 15,000 candles float on the lake, they nestle in egg shells saved at there.

ZaZiv Vegan Restaurant

Ljubljanska cesta 4, 4260 Bled, Slovenia Phone: +386 4 1 643 531

I am a committed carnivore. It is unlikely that anything would lead me to veganism, except this place. Their vegan burgers are among the best burgers I have ever tasted, better than any meat burger, prepared more expertly and comparatively well priced. I recommend it very highly. It is in the shopping centre.

Bar Planinček

Prešernova cesta 11 4260 Bled

This is a little bar and café hidden in plain sight between a bakery and the Fire Station (Gasilski dom). It is close to the bus station and the lake and is the best value for money for both coffee and beer.

K-Bar

Ljubljanska cesta 7, 4260 Bled, Slovenia Phone: +386 31 382 055

Even though it is in the Hotel Krim building beside the EuropCar hire office and a hairdresser, K-Bar is a little off the beaten track. It is a cool and shaded place with good, value for money coffee and croissants (rogljički) in the morning.

The little coffee shop at Infocenter Triglavska roža Bled

Ljubljanska cesta 27, 4260 Bled

I don't know if it has a name. It is small, the choice is limited, but it is charming and the setting is excellent. Checkout the centre – but take some coffee and cakes.

Gostilna Zatrnik Pr' Jagru

Zatrnik-Hrnica 82, 4247 Zg. Gorje

This is really something different. If you are a hiker, you might just come across this fascinating place on your walks. You might drive by on your way to or from Pokljuka. On the road, almost in the middle of nowhere (it is in fact near quite a lot of places, but somehow seems remote) this restaurant is famous for its hog roast. Suckling pig on a spit, very large helpings. Not a place to bring a vegetarian. Superb, rustic, authentic. Check the website for directions and menus [www.gostilna-zatrnik.si/].

20 recommended restaurants

These are in addition to the places mentioned above. Much as I would like to be able to boast that I've eaten in every restaurant in Bled, I have not managed that, yet. Here is a list of restaurants that I can recommend because either I have eaten there or they command a good reputation.

Restaurant Sova Bled

cesta Svobode 37, 4260 Bled, Slovenia Reservations: +386 59 132 100 info@restavracija-sova.com - www.restavracija-sova.com

Sova is a newish addition to Bled hospitality and it has quickly become one of my favourites. It replaced the Pletna Pizzeria on the lake shore at Mlino with a mid-range price but a fine dining eating experience in very informal surroundings. The food is largely modern Slovenian. The Sova Krožnik, is similar to a Balkan grill, but more sophisticated. They have a small but very good wine selection.

Pension Mlino

45

cesta Svobode 45, 4260 4260 Bled, Slovenia Phone: +386 4 574 14 04 mlino@mlino.si – www.mlino.si

This is a place for excellent traditional Slovene food (and Gorenjska music playing in the background). Although there are other restaurants in the building, the bar is the place to drop in for a drink or food. You will find it right opposite the pletna pier in Mlino. This is where the pletnar gather after their shift. Once again, a personal favourite for lunch, dinner or just a bowl of mushroom soup on a cold day. In summer, it can become very busy as the tour buses disembark their passengers at that point.

If there are two of you who like fish, the fish feast is one of the best items on the menu.

Restavracija Okarina

Ljubljanska cesta 8, 4260 Bled, Slovenia Phone: +386 4 574 14 58 leo@orarina.com - www.okarina.com/en/ Opening hours: Seasonal - 12am–11pm not open year round.

Once again, a favourite. This is the restaurant that shares its name with the world/ethno music festival held annually in Bled. You should expect in addition to the usual, good vegetarian food and spicy Indian food. Leo the owner is a vegetarian who visits India every year. Paul McCartney visited, he liked it.

Oštarija Peglez'n

cesta Svobode 19, 4260 Bled, Slovenia Phone: +386 4 574 42 18

Before we visited, people had recommended Oštarija Peglez'n for the fish, but there is a lot more to this lovely restaurant. Our first visit was 2014, then in July 2015. Summer 2015 was a blisteringly hot summer in Bled so the blinds were down in the terrace part of the restaurant which is the best place to sit in this weather. The light streams through, but we were protected from the strong rays. Two courses each, plus wine plus drinks to start - less than €30 per person which is good value for an excellent dinner. It is probably a little more expensive in 2017, but not significantly I hope.

Babji zob

cesta Svobode 8, 4260 Bled, Slovenia Phone: +386 8381-0584
info@ostarija-babjizob.si - http://www.ostarija-babjizob.si/en

The restaurant is named after the great rock by the Jelovice plateau "Babji zob" or "Old hag's tooth". Simple food, lots of Balkan grill meets and very large portions. In the summer time the terrace is busy and in the winter the bar-restaurant is warm, cosy and welcoming. Very good value of money and excellent food.

Hotel Jelovice Restaurant

cesta Svobode 8, 4260 Bled, Slovenia Phone: +386 4 5796 523
restavracija@hotel-jelovica.si - http://hotel-jelovica.afna.si/en/

With so many places for dinner that share a building with the hotel, it might escape your attention there is a restaurant inside. Unpretentious, simple and good value for money, the restaurant offers an evening self-service buffet for dinner between 19.00 and 21.00 with a table d'hôte (fixed price) menu including two starters, two soups, four main courses, four side dishes and a salad buffet plus a choice of deserts and wine, beer and juices and fruits.

Amazingly this is only €15. And it is very family friendly with great staff.

Restavracija Vila Ajda Dax

cesta Svobode 27, 4260 Bled, Slovenia Phone: +386 4 576 83 20
info@vila-ajda.si - www.vila-ajda.si/

One of the best known buildings in Bled – a lake-side 19th century villa – with international and Slovene cooking.

Vila Prešeren

Veslaška promenada 14, 4260 Bled, Slovenia Phone: +386 4 575 25 10 vila.preseren@sportina-turizem.si - www.villa-preseren.com/

Drop by for coffee after shopping or a beer after a walk around the lake which can turn into a full-scale lunch or even dinner. No more than a patch of grass and a pathway separates Vila Prešeren from the lake. Coffee cakes and drinks are good. Lunch – often specialities from Bled and Slovenia – is one of the best in the town. Although I've never been to dinner, the menu would suggest this is not a place for people on a tight budget.

Vrtnarija - Garden Village

cesta Gorenjskega odreda 16, 4260 Bled. Phone: +386 (0) 838 99 221
restaurant@gardenvillagebled.com - https://gardenvillagebled.com/

The 'GREENHOUSE' restaurant at Garden Village boasts "Slovenian Cuisine 'VRTNARIJA' - FRESH FROM OUR GARDEN TO YOUR PLATE"

Vrtnarija is among the most interesting and innovative restaurants in Bled. Situated in Mlino about 200m from the lake, it creates its own unique style bringing the outside, inside. The Garden Village "glamping" site opened in 2014 and the restaurant is part of this new development.

Yes, that is real grass growing (and carefully tended) on the tables – bringing a whole new meaning to "Surf and

Turf" (as if they served anything so ordinary). And that is little stream running through the restaurant and a tiny foot bridge to cross it. The first time we ate there was just a simple lunch – sandwich and a glass of wine by the pool. It was terrific.

The second time we visited was with a couple of local VIPs and we had the Chef's Tasting Menu. It was delicious. The food is unmistakably Slovenian – but modern and looks as good as it tastes and the bill matches the high standard.

Restavracija Grill

Best Western Premier Hotel Lovec Ljubljanska 6 4260 Bled, Slovenia Phone: +386 (0) 4 620 41 26 reservations@kompas-lovec.com - http://www.grill-bled.com/

The Grill serves some very good food. It is unlikely that you will be disappointed. We have only been there twice. The service was efficient.

Hint: better in than out. With the town's shopping centre and car park to one side and the busy main road to another, this is not the quietest or most romantic spot in Bled. Inside is a lot more comfortable.

The BBQ burgers, while not prominent on the menu, are excellent. The burgers are usually one of the features of the Taste of Bled exhibition held during the summer. The meat for the patties, the chef told me, is sourced from a nearby farm.

There is a strong traditional Slovenian theme to their menu. Each Thursday, from 15 June to 21 September at 7:00 pm they hold a Slovenian speciality event. Their example menu prices are mid-range.

Vila Bled

cesta Svobode 26, 4260 Bled, Slovenia Phone (0) 4 575 37 10 vila-bled@brdo.si - https://www.brdo.si/en/vila-bled/vila-bled

Vila Bled has had an interesting history. Before the building that sits on the land now, there was a grand castle. It was pulled down – reports from the time said the men working on the site had tears in their eyes as they destroyed the building. Post WWII this was summer home of President Tito. After Slovenia's independence, it became a hotel - part of a French chain - and is now owned by the Slovenian government.

The hotel gets all the reviews - and generally very high scores. The restaurant, which is excellent, tends to be overlooked by reviewers. Yes, it is expensive, one of a clutch of restaurants in Bled that will put a dent in your credit card. Overall, Slovenia is not an expensive place to dine and in that context, Vila Bled is expensive. Yet compared with a similar standard restaurant in most European capitals, it is exceedingly good value.

If you are on a budget, try lunch on the terrace on a sunny afternoon. The views are stunning - island, church, castle, pletna, St Martin's, and the edge of town. Full list. We love it. Even if you are not planning to use the restaurant, Vila Bled should be on your list of places to see. The extensive grounds are open to the public and are very pleasant for an amble. Parts, beyond the Belvedere Café are now abandoned and overgrown, including what I am told was once a private zoo.

Inside the hotel there is a small display of photos of world leaders who stayed there during Tito's time along with Tito's desk. Today some world leaders - or at least European leaders - still stay at the hotel; Bled is often the venue for major regional political events including Bled Strategic Forum.

Park Restaurant and Café

cesta Svobode 15, 4260 Bled, Slovenia Phone: +386 4 579 18 18 www.sava-hotels-resorts.com/en/bled/gastronomy/park-restaurant-and-cafe-

This is the home of the legendary Bled Cream Cake which is celebrated here when the town's summer season officially begins. Yes, a cream cake party. Often in the evening during the summer, there is live music.

The terrace views are great; the castle, the lake and the island. The seating is comfortable and the atmosphere outside is very pleasant. You are seated and served quickly. The staff are usually friendly, and efficient. However, in recent years, they have become stretched and while your order arrives quickly it can take time attracting attention to get your bill before you leave. If you are not staying long, ask for your bill with your order.

When it is busy I prefer to sit inside the restaurant. The coffee is good, the lunchtime sandwiches are good and reasonably priced. You still have the views from behind the glass. On a hot day, it is a good place to escape to.

Pri Planincu

Grajska cesta 8, 4260 Bled, Slovenia Phone: +386 4 574 16 13

Yes, this is the same Pri Planincu featured in Best Bar and Best Pizza, and no they are not paying for favourable reviews nor feeding me for free. It just happens this is my favourite place. The restaurant is old and a bit faded – that's why I like it. The food is traditional Slovene homemade fare and is consistently good (I've been eating there for over 20 years). If you grandmother was Slovenian, this is what her home would be like ... possibly. It is excellent for budget travellers, but you find plenty of people arriving in big cars eating there too.

More of the best

This is not "the best of the rest", because I know that many below are outstanding and could top any list. But, I have not been to any of them and can't give a firsthand account.

Both

Penzion Mayer

Želeška cesta 7, 4260 Bled, Slovenia Phone:: +386 4 576 57 40 http://www.mayer-sp.si/

and

Penzion Berc

Želeška cesta 15, 4260 Bled, Slovenia Phone: +386 4 574 18 38 http://www.penzion-berc.si/si

are nearby each other and close to Garni Berc which is consistently voted best place to stay in Bled – I've stayed; it is. Both have outstanding reputations and are in a beautiful setting away from all the crowds and the lake and near the Golf Hotel.

Gostilna Murka

Riklijeva cesta 9, 4260 Bled, Slovenia Phone: +386 4 574 33 40 http://www.gostilna-murka.com

Established in 1906 in the old part of town. It has a good reputation for traditional cooking and entertainment. A simple Slovene dinner will be inexpensive. The restaurant is "in the round" and is bright and airy on a warm evening. Excellent service.

Bled Castle Restaurant

Grajska cesta 61, 4260 Bled, Slovenia Phone: +386 4 620 34 4 www.jezersek.si/en/locations/bled-castle/bled-castle-restaurant

The Caste Restaurant has the reputation of being one of the top restaurants in all of Slovenia. There is no question that it has the best view.

Restavracija Arbor

Ljubljanska cesta 4, 4260 Bled, Slovenia Phone: +386 4 574 30 33 http://www.arborbled.si/about-arbor

In the shopping centre this looks like a very attractive simple restaurant with a big choice of Slovene and Mediterranean food on a well-priced menu. I notice they do pizza. It is on my list of places to test.

Restaurant 1906

Hotel Triglav, Kolodvorska 33, 4260 Bled, Slovenia Phone: +386 (0)4 575 26 10 info@hoteltriglavbled.si - www.hoteltriglavbled.si/en/restavracija-1906-bled

High above Bled overlooking almost the whole lake from Triglav Hotel. Modern Slovene cooking and Slovene wines. It has an outstanding reputation.

Restavracija Julijana

Toplice Hotel cesta Svobode 12, 4260 Bled, Slovenia Phone: +386 4 579 10 00

I have not had dinner or lunch there, but if you are feeling flush, they do a magnificent breakfast before 9.30 am

Slovenian wine

Slovenians are very proud of their wine and rightly so. St. Martin's Day is 11th November and is celebrated throughout the country as the day grape juice turns to wine. Most weekends in November, towns in and away from the wine growing regions hold events where you can sample new wines. Growers and producers set up stalls in St. Martin's Day Walks. You hire a glass from the organisers, buy a ticket or tickets and sample as many wines as you like. Simple traditional food is usually available like ričet – a thick barley soup. There is a St. Martin's Day celebration in Bled Castle each year, with traditional dancing and storytelling. And lots of tasting ... and food. Another is held in Spa Park (usually on a different day – so you get two cracks at sampling the wine).

Two other events worth knowing about are in Kranj where the St. Martin's Walk is held in the underground tunnels beneath the city. Around 3,000 people visit each year. The Ljubljana event is held over and around the Triple Bridge. Frankly, if you are looking for an excuse for a late autumn or early winter break, here it is. The weather is often overcast. Tiny puffs of cloud float between the hills and dodge the lake. It is a big public party, dignified, polite and very friendly. However, there have been postponements and cancellations of events when the weather forecast is particularly bad. Best to aim for venues where there is some cover – Bled and Kranj.

There are around 28,000 wine growers in Slovenia – we will pause for a second for you to re-read that. Surprising, isn't it? Most people do not think of the country as a wine producer. Yet there are three wine regions: the Drava, the Lower Sava, and the Slovene Littoral. They are all no more than the three-hour drive from Bled – they are all beautiful, breath taking and stunning. And Slovenia is one of the few regions of the world that produce ice wine.

If you enjoy wine, choose Slovenian first in a restaurant. Buying by the bottle? Aside from the supermarkets there are at least three wine shops in Bled. My choice is Vinoteka Zdravljica where you can sit and try before buying. The staff are lovely and just want you to enjoy their wine.

Some people might reserve half a day for the trip around the lake, another a day for the castle, another a day to walk in the hills. I suggest you reserve an afternoon (and possibly the evening) to take a wine tour of Slovenia from a chair at Vinoteka Zdravljica.

Alternatively, every Thursday at 5:00 pm (May to November) at Hotel Triglav's, wine cellar, there is a guided wine tasting. It lasts an hour or ninety minutes and costs €25. Triglav claims to be the only wine cellar in the region and with more than 150 Slovenian wines. You will taste wines from all over the country. You can get more details from the Hotel Triglav website [http://www.hoteltriglavbled.si/en/restavracija-1906-bled/vino]

Bled – Insider Knowledge

"About half an hour's drive from Bled is the Triglav Pokljuka Sports Centre and Hotel."

(Triglav National Park, Srednja vas v Bohinju 165a, 4267 Srednja vas v Bohinju, Slovenia).

"You will get a good lunch there any day, in the winter there is skiing and biathlon, but in the spring through to the autumn there are magnificent forest walks. There are mushrooms to pick (if you know what you are doing). Wonderful to spend a day among the trees."

Annika Novak

PART 5 – PEOPLE IN BLED

While the countryside around Bled is beautiful and the lake is "magical" (I did read one reviewer say that it is not "magical enough" and was left thinking about how one measures "magic"), when you get to know some of the people who live there, you really appreciate what makes the town special. Here are a few people I am fortunate to have met. Many more are quoted elsewhere in this book.

Župan (Mayor) of Bled

Profile – Janez Fajfar, the man who represents Bled to the world and at home.

For over 10 years, Janez Fajfar has been mayor of Bled, the Župan. Apart from his formal duties as the person who runs the town and plans its development, Janez can be seen at almost every event throughout the year, often welcoming tourists and VIPs. Sometimes he even goes back to his teenage years as a tour a tour guide and picks up the microphone to give a commentary as special guests are taken around town.

Professionally and not so co-incidentally his background is in the hospitality industry. Once the manager of Vila Bled, his childhood was spent in the company of other children from abroad when their families stayed with his in rooms rented to tourists.

Always charming, always entertaining, Janez and I have had many long meandering conversations. But for this, to keep us both focused, I asked him to answer a questionnaire. His story is fascinating.

He tells us about his past, the many famous people he has met, his hopes for the future and his legacy when he retires.

How long have you been mayor?

Since 2006

What does a mayor do?

It would be much easier to ask what he doesn't do.

With such a long history, are there historic ceremonial duties?

There are no special historic ceremonial duties, but some have been introduced [over the years]. The nicest is the pruning of the castle vine plant, a cutting, a "baby" of a 400 years old vine from Maribor, and cutting of the ripe grapes in autumn, of course.

Do you have duties at the castle, too?

When we have a special guest or just for fun I put on my burgundy coat with the black hare collar and fur cap with a peacock feather and the shiny mayor's chain, of course. Groups from the Far East drop by, all wanting a picture with me and my costume. I have to address numberless delegations and groups and give them a short talk on the past and present of Bled, if possible in a humorous way.

Who are some of the famous and important people you have met?

I am still meeting lots of them. Whenever someone important visits Slovenia, they normally come to Bled, too.

Being a tour guide as a student, then managing the Vila Bled, Tito's summer residence for 22 years and now more than 10 years a mayor, I've seen lots of dignitaries. The Queen with Prince Philip, Prince Charles, Prince Edward, just to mention the British, your numerous ministers, like Rifkind, Miliband.

Last year I enjoyed a lot the meeting with Bartholomeus of Constantinople, the world chief of the Eastern Orthodox Church. The most entertaining was the visit of the Spanish royal family, Queen Sofia asked her husband, King Juan Carlos to make a photo. The digital camera just came out, so he was not yet used to it. His royal spouse said to him as any other wife would do: "Is it even this you can't make?"

Mrs. Laura Bush also made a great impression on me, being so well read. Jeff Bridges, William Hurt, Michelle Pfeiffer, Michael Palin, Paul McCartney. Most of them can be really nice people, some cannot. Normally the more import they are, the fewer problems with them.

What did you do before you were mayor?

Before having my present post, I used to run Hotel Vila Bled, once Tito's mansion at the Lake Bled. The government opened it as a hotel four years after Tito's death in 1984. I stared as a reception manager and advanced to the manager in some years. In 1987 Vila Bled was accepted into the nicest hotel chain of the world, Relais & Châteaux. Our clientele was fabulous, very few snobs, mostly good old money, well behaved and respectful. Those who came to show off normally came just once, to the joy of the real ones. The City of London liked us a lot; I was even made a freeman in 2004.

The government rented the place for peanuts to a number of people who had no clue how to run a place like this and I just couldn't stand it anymore and decided to quit in the autumn of 2006. I just wanted to have a break in the winter to learn some of the excellent cooking of my 86 years old mother, retired chef. The municipal elections came in October, some friends finally convinced me to run for mayor and I got it... Now it is my third, four-year term.

Tell us about growing up in Bled

Growing in Bled was nice. We were not rich, but parents got a loan from the municipality to build a rather big home on the condition we rent some rooms to the tourists. I was just six years old when I sold the living

60

room to two Viennese, when my mother was shopping. We had to sleep in the cellar then.

As a child, I could meet many foreign children, we played together and subconsciously learned from each other. Sometimes they would take us with them to Holland for example; they sent us from one to another of the other people coming every year to my home, at the end some one of them would take us along driving to Bled to us, or to one of our neighbours.

Our home was like a railway station, always full of people, coffee, schnapps, salami, cake. Bled as a tourist place, attracted all sorts of people from anywhere. Children found some people to curious, unusual, so we gave remarks and got a slap from the parents.

We liked it a lot when Tito turned up with some exotic president or a royal. The school was out, the teachers sorted us along the main road, we got one of those colourful paper flags to wave when the endless line of the limousines passed by. The handles of the flags were the best materials for arrows for our cowboy and Indians battles.

What did your parents do?

We were a family of five; I was the middle one of three children. My mother was a magician of a chef. In the sixties and seventies guests were staying at our home on full board. We served about twenty people, also some tourists staying with our neighbours. So many dishes to wash and dry. My father was a mechanic, really widely known. He was always dressed in his blue overall, liked the cognac too much. Anyhow, police left him in peace, because they needed him more as he needed them. Both parents were good in several languages, something rather normal in a tourist place...

What are some of the best things about Bled?

The best thing is just to make an early morning or an evening walk the six kilometres around the lake, depend less of the weather or the season.

Do you have a favourite legend?

Definitely the legend of the sunken bell. (You can read about it later in the book.)

How many languages do you speak?

Next to the native Slovene, practised by just two million people, I learned the Serbo-Croatian; we started to learn English at school with eleven years. I picked up Italian and German from or guests, specially their children. I learned quite good French at the college, Polish as a side subject at University and some Spanish. I picked up Dutch as a tour guide on the bus.

When did you start learning languages?

I was always keen of music and wanted to understand what they sing. Being all the season with lots of foreign children, I learned the most of them.

What would you like to see happening in Bled in the future?

To be a bit political at the end: my first wish is for both very necessary bypass roads, the northern and the southern, they'll push the traffic away from lake. This will be the basis for an even better level of the tourists coming to Bled.

I'll do my best to keep Bled green and respecting our enormous natural and cultural heritage. I would also like to make Bled as good for our citizens as for the foreigners.

Insider Knowledge: What is the best thing you can do or see in Bled that tourists usually miss? What is the insider's secret about Bled?

Walking or taking a buggy ride through the nearby villages, climbing up Osojnica for the incredible view. Triglav National Park Information Centre.

Okarina Music Festival

Profile - Leo Ličof Founder and Artistic Director of The Okarina Festival

"I considered myself, even today, but back then when I was younger, to be a rare bird." Leo Ličof is founder and artistic director of the Okarina Festival which celebrated its 25th year in 2015. We met in his restaurant Okarina to look back at the festival's history and forward because even after all these years, Leo still has ambitions for the festival.

It all began appropriately enough with music, a trip to India and a restaurant specialising in vegetarian food. "I came back from India after I followed the Beatles example and had gone to Rishikesh." Rishikesh is in the foothills of the Himalayas and the place where Maharishi Mahesh Yogi trained The Beatles and others in transcendental meditation.

"I was inspired by so many bands playing good music." He grew up, like others of his generation around Europe, listening to Radio Luxembourg and to the Dutch Radio Veronica. "I found myself really frustrated behind an Iron Curtain. All these bands were "non-moral" or even "prohibited". I am mad about music – I love music. I played the violin – the fiddle. However, it was impossible in Yugoslavia at that time to create anything."

In 1991, everything changed. Slovenia withdrew from Yugoslavia, communist leaders throughout Central and Eastern Europe lost power and Leo seized the opportunity for his own revolution.

The toughest thing was getting the support.

"So, the first thing I did was to create the festival." The first festival was held two months after independence in the grounds of the restaurant Leo owned on the shore of Lake Bled not far where the Okarina restaurant is now.

There were only two or three bands on the bill. The next year was much the same and from there it began to grow.

"But, after the first three or four years of being independent, old powers started regaining political influence. And they did not like someone trying to bring this music "to our beautiful country". "Listen to our folk music," they told me. In their opinion this was a "strange guy bringing strange tunes." So, they gave me no support; not moral, not financial. I kept on going – and fortunately, there were many people around who were open minded."

Individual contributions from supporters kept the festival going. His butcher gave him a small contribution, his baker the same and with these small amounts he could book another band, and then with some more money, book another. He was hanging on to the festival by his fingernails. "Another mayor came along, who did not want the festival at all. I was told 'You have the right to do it – but don't come to me for support'.

"Then a different mayor came who was a bit more open minded and he gave 2 or 3 thousand pounds. But it was the moral support that gave me the strength to carry on."

Over its now 27 years, Okarina has been infused with local and national politics. But the whims of here today, gone tomorrow politicians have not dampened Leo's spirit or self-belief.

As he is talking we sip Indian tea, sweet and milky from the tea-pot. I notice in the background Joan Baez is singing Dylan's Forever Young. "I felt myself being a musical messiah. It was my duty to shake up a bit of consciousness of people in this region, to wake them up a bit.

"Then after 10 years I thought this is going nowhere ... 'Enough!' I thought."

There was no support financial or moral. So, there was no festival planned. "The mayor came to ask whether I would do the festival – I said no. But three weeks before the festival would have been due to start he came again pleading with me. 'I'll pay you – people are asking around.' Because after 10 years, people were beginning to think this is interesting."

Over the last eight years Zavod Za Kulturo Bled (the institute for Culture in Bled) has been financially supporting the Okarina festival and Leo especially mentions Špela Repnik, secretary of Zavod Za Kulturo, who helps to organize promotion, press conference and takes care of local transportation.

Even though one of his musical heroes, Paul McCartney visited the restaurant in 1985, his proudest moment is still the first year in the garden of the original restaurant. Hardly surprising. It was a wreck of a building which had been used as a restaurant. He and friends spent months clearing it out, cleaning it up, planting a garden where the first festival was held. They began to play music – mainly British and American – and added lots of vegetarian food to the menu. Leo ploughed all his profits right back into the restaurant. Standards improved –the restaurant became more popular. The diplomatic corps from Ljubljana were visitors as embassies with representation in the city became frequent customers. He planted a garden. "It was a natural amphitheatre. I put a fountain in the middle – parachutes above the garden for shelter and decoration, candles, and huge iron charcoal heaters." And that was where they held the first Okarina festivals.

The better the restaurant became, the more work and investment he put into it – and consequently – unfairly perhaps – the rent increased. Eventually it was ridiculous demands for rent that drove Leo from the original restaurant to where we were sitting.

Today, the Okarina restaurant is at Ljubljanska cesta 8. He combines running the restaurant with running the festival. Leo does almost everything himself. "I arrange everything from flights to t-shirts. Each band needs 30 or 40 emails forward and back." He also deals with all the contractual demands. "The band that has this requirement for staging, the band that has that needs conga drums to be supplied, this guy needs a flamenco guitar the other something else," Leo has been arranging all these years.

We finish our Masala Chai and I get ready to leave. Then in a sentence Leo encapsulated the idea of Okarina. "To create an atmosphere where people can start communicating – this is what we need most in the world, and in these mountains, even more."

For more information on the Okarina Festival, visit the website [www.festival-okarina.si/en/] and the Okarina restaurant is [www.okarina.com/en/]

Yoga Bled

Profile – Ana Pirih – Founder and organiser Yoga Bled

In the early morning, sometimes in the evening, if you are strolling around Lake Bled, you are likely to see a group of people immersed in concentration, eyes closed, bodies stretched. It is as likely as not to be a Popup Yoga session organised by Yoga Bled – and yes, anyone can join in.

Ana Pirih began organising Yoga Bled in 2015. "I'm licenced yoga instructor now and teach yoga almost every day," She tells me. "But I still study yoga, through workshops, books, articles and life that happens." She is the driving force behind the pop-up yoga sessions that are held on Lake Bled's shore.

She began the project with her partner and friend Maruša who was then the licensed yoga teacher. "Maruša is now just a guest teacher, because she doesn't have time anymore. So now I take care of everything – what goes on behind the scenes and at the class."

Yoga has been part of Ana's life for five years. "It has made a big difference to me. Even after the first year I noticed the difference, not just my body, but my mind as well. A lot has changed; my perspective on the world. Also, my body – how flexible I am and how I breathe and how I take things in life."

Ana uses one of the "four humours" to describe her temperament "I'm choleric." bad-tempered or irritable is another way of putting it. Although to be fair, she seems much more optimistic and energetic in person. "I was doing meditation and meditation brought me to yoga. With meditation and yoga I am more calm. If I look back a year – everything is different now."

The pop-up flow yoga sessions are open to anyone and held several times a week – check the Facebook page for details. "Flow is basically Vinyasa which is one of the many types of yoga. Vinyasa flow is a bit more dynamic. Hatha is a little slower – Vinyasa is much more connected to the integration of the breath and movement of the body. And asanas (the postures) are a bit more challenging. But it's OK for everybody from beginners to advanced yogis."

More than 150 years ago, a Swiss natural healer and physician Arnold Rikli arrived in Bled to recover from an illness. He decided Bled, and its environment, was a place of rare natural healing powers. He established one of Europe's healing centres here.

"I was studying Rikli when I was at the vocational school for tourism in Bled. I respect his work and ideas." Ana shares Rikli's belief that Bled has its own natural healing powers. "Maybe because of the water, maybe because of the air, maybe because it's not that hot, and maybe because of all of that – pointing out to the trees and plants on the lake shore – "because of all the green and the freshness."

Because Bled is such attractive place, the town can become crowded – particularly at weekends "My suggestion is to take a walk in Bled at 8:00 in the morning. There are few people and it is so fresh. That's when you will understand that Bled is a very healing place. Compared to the afternoon when no one says "Hi", tourists or locals. But in the morning, everybody says Hello. Good Morning. Živio!

We were sitting at the Devil Bar Caffe, late morning. Usually a busy part of town, but at this time of the day and this part of the week, it was as relaxed as any town can be. The Mayor walked by and waved greetings as he made his way to his office. "Saturdays and Sundays are packed - but this is Wednesday morning – it's peaceful. That's why I love this place do much."

Ana began practising yoga in Vila Viktorija. "I was thinking about how to bring yoga to more people, not just locals but tourists too, and came up with Yoga Bled. But more than bringing yoga to the locals and tourists, I wanted to bring the locations and this energy to everyone." The spark was ignited.

"Of course, if tourists come to our sessions then the sessions will be in English. Every week we are at a different venue. For the locals, these venues will repeat from time to time but for the tourists it will be something new every time. It's pop-up yoga. Every week yoga pops up at a different location."

Ana says that the yoga they do and the pace they take is suitable for everybody. "It doesn't matter if you are flexible, not flexible, what age you are. The importance of yoga, is that you begin. And if you have any problems you have to listen to your body. If your leg hurts you don't go into that asana yet. Just begin and practice, practice, practice and all is coming. If you practice you are going to bend, soon everything will come.

"Before yoga I was hyper-active, unable to completely relax. I could not have imagined myself doing this. I thought it was only for the flexible and for people who are calm and quiet and still – but yoga was exactly what I needed to calm down and be in the moment and just take time. to focus on the now. Today we are rushing from one place to another, we have so many social profiles and we are constantly typing and we don't find time to switch off and just be.

"That's what meditation and yoga can bring. Even if you don't want to try yoga, try meditation." And no better place than the quiet early morning shores of Lake Bled. "Just sit and just observe everything and that's it."

If you want to find out when the next Yoga Bled session will be held, and where it will pop up, you can get details from their Facebook page [facebook.com/yogabled] and the website is [www.yogabled.com].

Sessions normally cost €10 and includes the use of a yoga mat. You should book ahead by phone, or contact the team on Facebook and Twitter @YogaBled

Slovene Cuisine

Profile – Vlado "Dax" Dakskobler of Vila Ajda

Vila Ajda is one of the grand houses built in the 18th and early 19th century that are dotted around Lake Bled. It is now one of the best restaurants in Bled used by visitors and locals alike. For the last seven years, it has been run by Vlado Dakskobler.

"Everybody calls me Dax." He says as meets me at the restaurant reception on what is already becoming one of the hottest days of the year so far. We sit at a table on the terrace where we have two classic views of Lake Bled; the Castle and St. Martin's to my right and the church on the island in the distance directly in front.

Dax is enthusiastic about food, but he is even more enthusiastic about this town where he grew up and the region where is family is from. "It is one of the safest places in the world. You can walk around the lake at three in the morning with a thousand euro in your pocket, no problem."

The food is strongly Slovene and draws not only from the region but his own family. Dax talks me through the menu. He becomes more enthusiastic and passionate as he goes along.

The menu ranges from the humble Struklji (one of the most characteristic everyday Slovenian dishes, usually made from cottage cheese rolled-up in dough) and Balkan meats like Ćevapčići (grilled minced beef), and Ražnjići (skewered meats) through to Chateaubriand. But Dax points out Jelenov Medaljon (Deer Medallions) as one of the highlights for him.

Lunch starts with a selection of cold meats including pork salami, beef salami and tongue – light and full of flavour. The sourcing of local ingredients is emphasised in the menu whether that be mushrooms picked by local farmers or trout caught just a few kilometres away in the Sava River.

Dax trained formally, but he also inherited family skills. He mentions his grandmother several times during our conversation. "Knowledge passed on from one generation to another. This is the cuisine of the people of this area. But we are half an hour from Italy, half an hour from Austria, and over the last few hundred years found the best of the cuisine from those countries, too. And from Istria (the Slovene region to the west on the Adriatic). And we were part of Yugoslavia – so we have dishes from Yugoslavia." Slovenia is not generally regarded as part of the Balkans, but there is at times a strong Balkan influence on the food.

And the menu – which changes four times a year to reflect the season – uses ingredients and dishes from the wider geographical area with Italian and Austrian taking their place. Some dishes are from very specific areas such as Mojstrana and Dvoje, villages in the Alps between Bled and Kranjska Gora.

Main course arrives – a house special; pečene ripsi reba brez maščobe (literally ribs and veal shank baked without fat). It is served with roast vegetables – with a slight bite – in a pan which is at lunchtime probably enough for two people. Slovenian portions are often extremely generous.

"My grandmother cooked everything with fat – but I say we cannot do that. I like to be slim – and my customers like to be slim too. We use olive oil where she used fat. It is better for the food, better for you and me. We take the traditional foods but use modern techniques to make it healthier.

"I will cook anything for a customer. Sometimes I need some notice. When my grandmother cooked, she would open her cupboard and say "This I have. This I make." And maybe go to the shop once a month. For me I can call Australia, Africa, anywhere in the world to get ingredients to make dinner for my guests."

The waiter brings three bottles of Slovenian wine to try. Damski Rosé, a Kras Teran and a Cabernet Sauvignon Amfora. The house wine here is Erzetic, a family owned winery in Goriška Brda.

"The choice of house wine in Slovenia is very important." Slovenian wine is not well known beyond the region so part of the job of the Slovenian restaurateur is to help customers new to the country learn something about the local wine. "We are a country of two million people, but we have twenty-eight thousand wine growers."

We are heading for the dessert and Dax describes a special dessert he once made for a Thai princess which is now on the menu and photograph of her in the restaurant. Next to it – and on the other side of the social spectrum – is a photo of documentary film maker Michael Moore (Fahrenheit 9/11 and Bowling for Columbine) in the restaurant.

Dax is a powerfully positive individual; positive about what he has achieved and positive about Bled's future. "Look what I have done in the last 7 years. Why do some say, 'No is not possible.' Everything is possible."

Each year A Taste of Bled celebrates the cuisine from the area. In 2017, the food festival will be held during Bled Days and Bled Nights on 21 to 23 July. For more information contact TIC Bled Turistično društvo Bled, cesta Svobode 10 4260 Bled. Phone: +386 4 5741 122 email: info@td-bled.si

You will see Dax in Restavracija Vila Ajda Dax most days at cesta Svobode 27, 4260 Bled. Phone: +386 4 576 83 20 e-mail: info@vila-ajda.si [www.vila-ajda.si/]

Diving in Lake Bled

Profile – Matjaž Repnik, Diving Instructor

Matjaž Repnik has been teaching diving at Lake Bled for about three years. He and other enthusiasts also participate in the annual lake clean up. When I spoke to him in Mlino, near the pletna pier over a few bottles of Laško, he was preparing to pack up to go home after a long day in and on the lake.

Until 2010 Matjaž was working in IT in Radovljica a town with a beautiful old centre about 15 minutes away from Bled. He swapped his desk job for diving and is now a full-time instructor working in Bled, on the Slovenia coast and Croatia. During the winter in 2016 and 2017 he worked in Sri Lanka. Matjaž has made over 1,000 dives and is in (and under) the water six times a week during the summer.

"Lake Bled has around six different diving spots. It is biologically diverse and interesting," Matjaž tells me. As we stood at the lake shore he talks about the variety of fish and fauna under the water. "There is something like eighteen different species in the lake. You will find carp, catfish, pike, zander, trout, perch and there are smaller species, too as well as the underwater plants." Almost every day of the year you will see anglers fishing from the shore, most staying awake overnight and making early morning catches. The biggest fish found in the lake was a common carp weighted 30.7 kilograms and was about 2 metres long.

The water lilies are just beginning to come alive on the surface of the water as we look out across the lake. "The visibility is pretty good at about 3 metres. We dive only to 10 metres. But the lake goes down to 30 metres where visibility is zero and temperature is only 6 degrees."

At its longest, Lake Bled is 2,120 m (6,960 ft) and widest at 1,380 m (4,530 ft). It attracts swimmers from around the world, some because of the potential healing qualities of the water. In high summer the lake temperature can reach over 21c. This lake and the climate attracted Arnold Rikli to Bled 160 years ago. Rikli was a Swiss natural healer and physician. He proposed various therapies, mostly based on exposing the body to sun and air. He was among the first people who noticed the healing effect of the natural environment in Bled

"The Discover Scuba Diving course is an elementary introduction to scuba diving. I take only two people at a time. They get a taste of the excitement and the experience. They won't see everything hidden under the surface in one or two dives, but it does give novices the opportunity to taste the experience."

Divers also help keep the lake clean. "Twice in its history, Lake Bled has been close to death, almost killed off by algae." Significant steps were taken a few decades ago to ensure the health of the lake. "Last Saturday," says Matjaž, "Was Cleaning Day for the lake. Divers came from all over Slovenia. I was helping clean just where we are now in Mlino."

What did they find down there? "I couldn't bring out part of a car engine! There was an old toilet and crockery. Each diver brought out a huge bag of rubbish."

Sadly, even though there is a medieval castle and an ancient church on Lake Bled and a civilisation of over 1000 years, Matjaž has not yet found any lost treasure. About a centimetre of silt forms on the bottom of the lake every year and over time any "treasures" have either been found or covered up by nature. Or perhaps were never there at all.

Watching a film about diving changed his career path and his life. "In the village where I am from in the Culture Centre, people give photo presentations and talks about places they have been. One guy had been to Mexico and had made an underwater movie. As I watched, I saw the bubbles created by the divers breathing apparatus. I had never seen anything like that before. I was inspired by those bubbles."

The decision to be a diving instructor was made. From Slovenia, Matjaž headed to Gran Canaria to train and to work for 3 months. He moved on to Croatia where he qualified as a diving instructor. Once qualified he moved to Malaysia for seven months and worked as diving instructor. Then back to Slovenia and Austria where he now works full time and has founded his own diving club.

"I am a PADI instructor and a course here in Bled or in Slovenia is recognised anywhere in the world. The Discover Scuba Diving course is a onetime event, but if someone wants to do something more advanced I can do that with them. Next level is an Open Water Course. You can come here and do that in three or four days. There are dives and skills and safety training. And I teach you to navigate under water with a compass. After that you can dive up to 18 metres anywhere in the world. If you are already a diver and are looking for a dive buddy, if you bring your certification we can dive together.

"Today I was running a Rescue Course and some tourists from the Netherlands stopped when they saw the equipment and they wanted to know about diving in Lake Bled. I explained the way I am explaining to you. So now I am going to be organising a dive for them."

For more information or make a booking you can contact Matjaž via his website http://watersports.si/en/contact Or email him ahead of your visit to Slovenia at info@watersports.si

Bled - Insider Knowledge:

I like the walk on little hill called Dobra Gora altitude 625m . From where I live I walk in the direction of direction Dinol (part of the town) south east. It is about 1h to walk from my house. The climb takes about 25-30 min. It is pretty steep but on top is stunning view on Jelovice area and Ribno village. It is never crowded with people. Even locals don't go to much.

Luka of Hotel Garni Berc

Voted Tripadvisor's "Best Hotel in Bled" many years in succession.

PART 6 – STORIES AND IDEAS

The Historic Pletna Boats

One of the great attractions for almost every visitor to Bled is the short voyage to and from the island on a pletna boat. They are unique to Bled. Why are they here at all?

Standing on the stern of the pletna, the skipper – "pletnar" – rows his 20 passengers to Bled Island. The passengers, protected from the sun (or the rain) by the colourful awning sit low enough to dip their fingers in the lake. The pletna and pletnar are unique to Bled and are one of the enduring symbols of the area. The pletnar you see is likely to have built or helped build his flat-bottomed boat. And he – they are all men – is part of a family tradition going back almost 1000 years.

The story of the pletna boat is believed to start about 1150. The land around the hamlet Mlino on the southern coast of Lake Bled was not good enough to farm. So, families in the village were given permission from the local authorities to ferry pilgrims to the island. It was a way to make a living, but also an effective way for the authorities to raise taxes.

In the reign of Empress Maria Theresa (who ruled from 1740 to 1780), twenty-two families were given exclusive rights to transport pilgrims to the island. Three centuries later, descendants of those families are still the exclusive operators of the pletna boats.

Pletna Today

According to Marjan Zupan a pletna skipper in Mlino, the distinctive style of the modern day pletna was decided in the early 20th century. He writes about it on his website [pletnaboat.com] "Significant changes in building a pletna boat came in the year 1902 when it got the shape it has today. The most credit for that goes to my grandfather Anton Zupan who was involved at the construction of the pletna boat." The vessel measures 7 metres by 2 metres transports up to 20 passengers.

There are some old black and white photos of pletna boats and of old Bled on the exterior wall of the fire station in Mlino.

Web Links

- Pletna skipper Marjan Zupan has written about their history on PletnaBoat.com.
- You can make bookings for groups and events here at Pletna.si
- There is also information on the Bled.si website and WikiPedia.

The legend of the Wishing Bell

There is a story about a special bell – one that cannot be seen, but sometimes is heard. The story says that it is somewhere under the lake's waves, near the island.

The bell was being transported to there and during a storm the boat carrying it sunk and was never seen again. The story is remembered every Christmas Day with an exhibition of lights, dance and fire, because it was no ordinary bell.

Legend has it that around the year 1500 a bell had been commissioned by the wife of the Master of the Castle after he had gone missing, presumed dead. When she heard about his disappearance, Hartman Kreigh's wife Poliksena was so distraught that she gathered all the gold and silver in the castle collection to pay for a new bell for the island church so that he would be remembered every time it rang. As much as his wife loved him, Kreigh was mourned by few others. Farmers had complained about him trampling on their rights and humiliating them. He was reviled by the people of Bled. Some people thought that his "disappearance" might have been at the hands of the enemies he had made in the rural community.

The bell was cast, but as it was being transported to the island, the weather changed dramatically, and a storm began whipping the waves of Lake Bled into a final revenge on Kreigh. The boat became unstable and the bell fell into the water sinking into the lake bed's mud never to be seen again. They say even today, it still sometimes heard ringing from the depths of Lake Bled.

The Wishing Bell which now rings out from the church is a replacement sent by the Pope of the time. It is a tradition to ring the bell to wish and for good fortune. Ring the bell and you will again make your way back to Bled.

Bled Island – its history and traditions

People have lived in this area since the Mesolithic times (5,000 to 10,000 BC). It is not difficult to imagine that even from the earliest times it was regarded as a spiritual place. In pre-Christian times, it was a place of pilgrimage and sacrifice. People have been visiting the island to worship from pre-history right up to the present day. Although there are more tourists than pilgrims today.

There is evidence of settlements in the area from stone age, iron age and Roman times. Graves from around 600 BC have been found. The pre-Christian era ended in the 7th century. For some time, the island had been the place of worship to the goddess Živa. With the Slavic settlement, around 600 AD, and the conversion from pagan to Christian, worship of Živa was replaced by devotion to the Virgin Mary. Parts of the present day church link back to the 15th century.

Today, weddings are celebrated in the church and occasionally Masses are said. There has been an annual concert by the wives and mothers of the Pletnars.

Getting there by Pletna is the traditional journey.

The entrance to the Church and Bell Tower is Adults €6.00, Students €4.00, Children €1.00 and Family ticket €12.00. According to the island's website "The only way to access Bled Island is by taking a Pletna - a handmade wooden boat propelled by a Pletnar who rows standing up." A pletna trip is €12 per person. You will be able to stay only half an hour. Whether you think 30 minutes is long enough to visit the island and appreciate the spiritual nature of the place is up to you. I find it all a bit of a rush.

There are five locations around the lake where you can board a pletna. They are not always staffed. The most popular places are on the boardwalk behind Hotel Park and beside Hotel Prešeren. The pier at Mlino is normally used for organised trips although you can sometimes get on board there. There is also a departure point in Velika Zaka, but it is not available year-round.

It is possible to hire a rowing boat to get to the island. Places to dock are limited. Take advice when you are renting. In 2016, a modern electric driven pletna was introduced causing great controversy and unrest with the traditional boatmen pulling their craft out of the water in protest. Eventually the dispute was resolved. At time of writing I have no information as to whether the service will be available in 2017.

There is more information on the Bled Island website [www.blejskiotok.si] Email: info@blejskiotok.si. Phone: +386 4576 79 79☐

Seven things to do before 7:00am

Venture out before early breakfast and around the lake you will see photographers, people fishing, power walkers and the first pletna taking staff to the island. Are you ready to start your day good and early? These are only 7 things you can do around Lake Bled, breakfast not included.

1.   The Bells. The Bells.

Make your way to the boardwalk near the main camping site a little before 7:00 any morning. It is probably about a 40 minute walk from the town centre, almost half way around the lake. There won't be many people about. It is not silent - there is plenty of birdsong, the occasional quack, the odd cyclist and a runner or two.

From there you can see the island, the castle and St. Martin's church. During the summer months, you will also enjoy the sunrise. Then a few seconds before 7:00am, a bell tolls, then another, and the sound builds. Some of the peals are from the Church of the Assumption on the island, others from St. Martin's, but there are other, more remote bells ringing, too.

They all welcome a new day and peal for about four minutes, Good morning Bled.

2.   Biking, running, walking - just because it's fun

This is by far the best time to put on your trainers and get the best from running, walking and cycling around the lake, and even further. Later in the day the cyclists tangle with walkers on the paths. The runners will face walkers coming in the opposite direction. But now, there are so few people around the lakeside is all yours. The round lake route is a good 90-minute walk or 25 minute bike ride, but why not go further?

3.   Sunrise Lake Bled

You don't have to be active and energetic to enjoy the morning. Just find a bench and enjoy the air, the sounds and the clear light. The south west part of the lake is the best spot for watching the sun come up behind the hills. When and where is the best sunrise? See next.

4.   See the pink cloud factory at work

In the autumn, something magical happens. As the sun emerges from behind the hills, it warms the lake and the mist rises. The sun shines through the mist turning it from white to gold to yellow to pink. This is the time to take some amazing photos of the colourful mist swirling around the lake and up into the air towards the castle. It is a stunning sight. Best place to view it is probably at Zaka near the camp site.

5.   Swim

There is no better way to start a summer's day in Bled than a swim in the lake. The water is warm and deep and there are many secluded corners for the shy swimmer to strike out into what many believe are healing waters. Healing or not, you will feel so much better after floating on your back watching the whips of clouds drift by above you.

6.   A barefoot walk

During the summer, there is an organised barefoot walk and you can join a group of people enjoying the dew between their toes. There is no need to wait for an organised walk. Enjoy the open fields and pastures alone or with your own group of friends.

People have come to Bled for generations to enjoy the health-giving properties of the region; the water, the air and even the soft cool grass on a warm summer morning.

The 19th Rikli's Walk to Straža hill will be at 7:00 am on 2 July 2017 meeting in front of Hotel Golf.

7.   Feed the ducks

Do not feed bread to the ducks and swans. We have all done it and the ducks seem to like it, but experts in duckie-culture advise us to vary what we give them and select healthier more natural treats like oats, corn, or defrosted frozen peas. And exercise portion control.

It is a wonderful sight to watch the ducks fly in from the other side of the lake, and scoot over the water as they land and all for some free food. If you are in one of the wider open grassy spots like Mlino in the early morning, you will see ducks and swans on the bank tugging at the grass and feeding themselves and preening in the early sun rays.

10 "Must Dos" in Bled and around Lake Bled

Most of the ideas here are not new or original. If you spend a week in Bled, you will probably do most of them without thinking about it. But if you are off the train and heading next to Ljubljana, Croatia or somewhere else and you only have a short time, here are 10 top activities to try to give you a real taste of Bled.

1.   Head for the Information Centres

There are two Information Centres in Bled; one in the main shopping area near the Casino which you should make your priority, the other is Bled Tourism Office Infocenter Triglavska roža Bled, Ljubljanska cesta 27, 4260 Bled Phone: +386 (0)4 5780 205 e-mail: info@dzt.bled.si

You should go to both if you have time. They will bring you right up-to-date with what's going on in town and around the lake. If you are a serious hiker, outdoor sports fan, or planning a visit to the Triglav National Park, then the Infocenter Triglavska roža Bled is a must for information, maps, books and advice.

2.   Go Around Lake Bled At Least Once

The top modes of transport are:

Feet and legs – walking is easily the best way to get around the lake and to explore some of the places you'll miss by going at speed. Allow 90 minutes to 2 hours. But you can really extend it if you want to. There are many coffee and snack places to re-fuel or just sit and watch the day go by.

Tourist Train – It costs €4 and takes around 25 minutes. But you can hop on and hop off as often as you want to. There are stops including at Mlino, Zaka (near the large camping site), beside the boat club, near St. Martin's church and three of four places to climb aboard in town. The train departs about every 45 minutes. Check the time tables at the stops.

Bicycle – Hire a bike if you want to cover a lot of ground independently. A quick once around the lake takes 25 – 30 minutes. But try to avoid busy times of the day. Cyclists are not greater beings than other visitors, they have no priority, even though some think they do. It is astonishing how rude many cyclists are to walkers. The trip is not all flat but it is not a challenging ride. There is information about bike hire elsewhere in this book.

Horse drawn carriage – This is going to cost €40, but up to 4 people can travel together. The journey takes about 25 to 30 minutes. You will find the coachmen (fijaker) beside Festival Hall. They will take you to other destinations including the Castle. There is a list of destinations and prices.

3. Visit the Island

It is an experience. Some people do it every visit, for others once is enough. The most common ways to get there are:

By Pletna – These are the flat-bottomed boats. The return fare is €12. There are piers at 5 points around the lake. It is a lovely trip, however once you reach the island, might want more than 30 minutes there. Talk to your Pletnar before departing to find out if you may return in a different boat. (The Pletnar is the pletna captain.)

Rent a boat and row which will cost around €12 per hour. The advantage with rowing is that you decide timings, and there is a place to tie up on the island. The disadvantage is ... well you have to row. Take advice when you are hiring about rules for docking at the island.

You could swim, but if you want to go into the Church you'll need to wear more than Speedos.

Why go? Lots of reasons -

- Climb the 100 steps - or get someone to carry you.
- Visit the church - ancient and graceful.
- Climb the clock tower.
- Ring the Wishing Bell.
- Different views across the lake.
- Find a quiet corner and think or meditate.
- Visit an exhibition.
- Get the T-Shirt (literally). There is a shop on the island with some very nice collectables.

4. Eat Lunch

You can go from 5-star grandeur at the more expensive hotels to a tuna roll from Mercator sitting on a bench beside the lake.

My tip – Burek from Pekarna Planika (Triglavska cesta 43, 4260 Bled). This is a fantastic little bakery open from 6:00 am. Burek is a term than encompasses a range of traditional food. In this case, it is crumbly pastry with various fillings such as potato and onion (krompir), cheese (sir), or mixed meats and for desert, apple. You will find it on the road from the bus station going towards town.

There is an extensive list of other places to eat in this book including many personal recommendations.

5.   Eat Cake

OK, it is easy to become controversial here. Bled cream cake is what everyone talks about. It is part of the marketing of the town – part of the marketing of Slovenia. Fair enough. You can get it almost anywhere – Park Hotel's Terrace has the history and the setting – but up past the bus station toward the Castle is Slaščičarna Šmon – possible the best pastry shop on the planet. They have Bled cream cake, too, but so much more.

The only way to know which is better is to try both; one in the morning the other in the afternoon. Other providers of Bled cream cake are available, everywhere.

6.   Head for higher ground

One of the first thing you will notice about Bled is that it is surrounded by hills. Each has a different stunning view of the lake.

Straža and Castle hills are both fairly accessible. Straža even has a chair lift to get you up and summer tobogganing to get you down. Summer tobogganing is excellent fun and should be separate on this list, but there is so much to fit in.

To get to Castle, you can climb a few hundred steps up the side of the hill if you are fit enough. Starting from the steps at St Martin's Church is probably easiest. You could walk from the bus station past the George Best Bar and up along the road. At times during the summer season, there is a bus. A taxi which will probably cost about €10 from the town centre. Entrance to the Castle is €9.

If you are fit enough and are prepared for a challenge you could try Osojnica the hill where some of the most famous photos of Lake Bled are taken. But it can be tough going if you have spent your working life behind a desk.

The last option is from the Bled Jezero train station. Nice view - not terribly high, though.

7.   Go Somewhere Else

If you are staying in Bled for more than a day, then Vintgar Gorge is a must. It's not too far to walk to, but there is a bus during the summer. The Hop On - Hop Off bus will take you to nearby villages and towns (if it is operating when you are there). Or you could use Bled as a base and turn to the next chapter for suggestions of other places to visit.

There are many marked and signposted walks. As you follow the paths you will see signs encouragingly pointing you in the right direction. You can find routes in "Bled – City Map" and "Bled – A Tourist Map" which you can get from Tourist Information and other tourism outlets.

There are guided tours including walking tours around the lake where an expert will point out things you might miss otherwise.

8.   Swim

Well, it's a lake, people have been coming for the water here for almost 200 years.

There are lots of swimming places around Lake Bled. There are lots of fishing places too, so be considerate. Where's best? The Public Lido is best if you like to have a place to store your clothes and there is a busy bar and restaurant adjacent. Mlino attracts sunbathers and swimmers, but getting in and out of the water is not quite so easy there. There are steps to ease yourself in. Zaka Camping also attracts sunbathers and families too. There is a pier to jump off, but it is easy just to walk into the water.

And the water itself? In the summer the water can get up to 30c I have been told. That might be an exaggeration but is comfortably warm at the height of the season. And there are people who swim in clubs during the coldest days of winter.

Best time in spring and summer for a quiet swim is always in the morning or in the evening when the crowds have gone. But even if you don't swim you can sit at the edge of the lake and dip your toes.

9.   St. Martin's Church

The church of the Assumption of Mary on the Island rightly gets a lot of attention. Whether you are a church goer or not, the parish church St. Martin's is a cool and shaded escape on a hot sunny day, or a place for quiet contemplation all year. Over Christmas there is a beautiful nativity scene.

In this region of Slovenia, there is no shortage of churches – big and small, by the road or high in the hills. There may be as many as 3,000 in the country. St. Martin's was built between 1903 to 1905. Among the beautiful frescos is one portraying Vladimir Lenin as Judas Iscariot in a depiction of the Last Supper. Do remember, this is a church where the faithful come to worship, not just on Sunday. So, be respectful.

10.   Start planning your return

This happens more often than you might expect, not for everyone, but half way through a visit, some people realise that there is more to see, do and experience than they had expected. For us it was "I wonder what the lake is like in the winter." If you are one of the many who are captivated, now is the time to think about what you are going to do on your return.

And book early. Once Easter passes, accommodation becomes more difficult to book for the summer. Bled is a 12-month destination, so other times of the year are easier – and less expensive – to book.

PART 7 – BLED AS A BASE

Usually, people make Ljubljana a base and take trips from there. Bled can also be a starting point for the whole of the Gorenjska region. There is not enough room here for an exhaustive list of all the places you can go, but here are a few ideas.

Insider knowledge -Triglav National Park

You could spend weeks in Triglav – a lifetime exploring. Tomaž Piber's has lived in Bled all his life, and the Piber family, for generations. His suggestion for his insider secret to Bled, takes us right out of the town and into the heart of the national park.

"If you are making a short visit, one place you could focus on is Pocar Homestead, a museum decorated house, considered one of the oldest homesteads in the park. You will find a rich collection, themed on life in the towns near Triglav over the centuries. During the summer months, the barn homestead event space is used for cultural and creative presentations."

Pocar Homestead is in Mojstrana, 30-minute drive from Bled or by bus via Lesce on the way to Kranjska Gora.

Open on Saturdays and Sundays and holidays from 11:00 am to 6:00 pm. Zgornja Radovna 25, SI-4281 Mojstrana. Phone 386 (0) 4 578 0200, 386 (0) 4 578 02

For more information and more detail on opening hours, check [www.kranjska-gora.si/en/sightseeing/cultural-sights/homesteads-and-houses/pocar-homestead] or call Kranjska Gora tourist information 386 4 580 94 40 e-mail: info@kranjska-gora.eu

Go to Italy for lunch

One of the most beautiful day trips from Bled is by train to Nova Gorica on the border with Italy. Not only are Nova Gorica (Slovenia) and Gorizia (Italy) attractive places to visit, the train journey itself is an experience.

The route begins at Jesenice railway station but you can join the train at Bled Jezero. The journey takes you through the historic Bohinj railway route. Following the Soča River most of the way, the train travels over high bridges, viaducts and through tunnels up to 6,000 metres long.

As you pass over the Solkan Bridge, you might not notice much except you are so high and there is a fabulous view. The view of the bridge, which you won't see from the train, is something special, too. Search the web for photos. Solkan Bridge is an astonishing and beautiful fete of engineering.

The 219.7 metre bridge over the Soča River is near Nova Gorica. With an arch span of 85 metres (279 ft), it was originally built between 1900 and 1905, and officially opened in 1906.

In the same year, the Bohinj Tunnel, which connected central Europe with Trieste, was opened by the heir presumptive to the Austro-Hungarian throne, Franz Ferdinand. At Bohinj station there is a small exhibition about the tunnel and the historic railway construction.

Nova Gorica and Gorizia

The train station is only a few metres from the Italian border and when you arrive you can choose which town to visit; the modern Yugoslavian/Slovenian Nova Gorica (a 20 minute walk) or the old Italian town Gorizia (a 30 minute walk).

"In 1947, following World War II, Italy signed a peace treaty with the Allies, including Socialist Yugoslavia. The treaty transferred most of the Slovene-inhabited

areas of the Italian Province of Gorizia to Yugoslavia. The town of Gorizia, itself, however, remained under Italian rule. The new border was drawn in a way that cut the city off its north-eastern surroundings, and left around 40% of the territory of the municipality to Yugoslavia, including the suburbs of Solkan, Šempeter, Kromberk, Rožna Dolina, and Pristava. The Communist authorities of the Socialist Republic of Slovenia therefore decided to build a new settlement in the area just along the new border, linking the former suburbs of Gorizia into a new urban space, named Nova Gorica or New Gorizia. The first projects were laid out in late 1947, and the construction began at the beginning of the following year.

Wikipedia [https://en.wikipedia.org/wiki/Nova_Gorica]

Once you have inspected the Italian Slovene frontier follow the road south (or turn left out of the station). You will be walking parallel with the border. At the T-junction turn right for Italy and left for Nova Gorica. Walk around, follow your nose – try to find the main square in Gorizia and if you want a stand-by recommendation for somewhere to have lunch, I've been to Pizzeria Al Lampione - Via Silvio Pellico 7 Gorizia, twice and enjoyed it both times.

You can go any day by the ordinary train service from Jesenice – which stops at Jezero Bled and takes a little under 2 hours. There is enough time to walk to either town for lunch. If you are planning a longer visit, check the timetables on the Slovenian Railways website.

The normal fare is €6.59 (Children aged 6 to 12, €3.30. The young persons' fare for people aged 12 to 26 is €4.61. You can also get a weekend return. Tourist return trip on weekends and public holidays is a fantastic deal €9.22 (prices correct as of 1 April 2017). Please check the Slovenian Railways website for any changes (but those prices have remained stable for at least 2 years).

The Heritage Train

As an alternative to scheduled journey, you can transport yourself back in time 100 years and try the Heritage Train package with departures in 2017 From Jesenice and Bled Jezero on May 6th, 20th, June 3st ,10th, 17th and 24th, July 8th, August 19th, September 9th, 16th and 23rd, October 14th, and November 4th. These stream-train trips are very popular and sell out early. Don't expect to turn up and buy a ticket. Advance seat reservations are required.

You will be accompanied by actors dressed in period costume including a couple portraying Franz Joseph and his wife.

More on the Slovenian Railway website. [www.slo-zeleznice.si/en/passenger-transport/around-slovenia/heritage-trains/take-the-heritage-train-along-the-bohinj-line]

An easy morning and lunch in Radovljica

Radovljica. The name looks like a mouthful. But really, it's not. Try "Radol'ca".

To get there take a short bus journey or even an off-road cycle ride. After the bus stops at Lesce, the Radovljica bus station is next. The old town is just past the DM chemist shop and across the car park. It is always busy around the bus station; anyone will point you in the right direction.

Why are we going there? First to look at the beautiful old buildings. Many have been renovated over the last few years restoring them to how they must have looked in the 15th and 16th century when they were built. The main street in the old town is short but manages to squeeze in two museums, two restaurants, a café, shops a church and accommodation, and more.

If you have a sweet tooth, then this is the place for you. Honey, honey bread, ginger bread and chocolate. There was a festival of chocolate in 2017 is on the weekend 21, 22 and 23 April 2017. Being so popular, you might well expect a repeat in 2018.

Gingerbread Museum and Workshop

In the basement of Gostilna Lectar, there is an authentic workshop where the famous gingerbread hearts are made. Gingerbread hearts are not unique to Radol'ca or even Slovenia, but here you can watch them being made and even (if you ask nicely) help in the process. It is great for adults – and tremendous for children. You can also buy honey bread.

The first gingerbread bakery was established here in 1766. In 1822, the owners opened the restaurant. In 2006, they renovated and opened the vaulted rooms as a working bakery. For more details and opening hours check the website [www.lectar.com].

The restaurant is very traditional and the food is excellent – my favourite is mushroom soup in a bowl of hollowed out bread.

Another excellent restaurant for lunch looking out over the hills behind the town is Gostilna Avguštin, Linhartov trg 15, 4240 Radovljica.

In 1996 when the now mayor of Bled told me there was a beekeeping museum in Radol'ca, I had no idea how important apiculture is in Slovenia and this region. There is a map in the museum showing that bees from the surrounding countryside have been exported to the world. In nearby Lesce there is the Gorenjska Region Beekeeping Development and Education Centre. In a world where bees are reportedly on the decrease, apiculture is a serious business. It is also an historic and colourful business. There is a wonderful display of all sorts of beehives and decorative panels collected over the centuries. The historic panels capture the history and the culture of the region. They show scenes of family life (not always "PC"), religion, superstitions and fears. There are beehives like intricate dolls houses. One is a wooden man at least 3 metres high. Modern hives have brightly coloured panels.

The Tourist Office can provide information and suggestions of even more places to see around this beautiful area. It is right at the top of the old town. Ask about the free sightseeing tour of Radovljica's Old Town which usually happens every Tuesday at 10.00 am. It I organised by Radovljica Tourist Information Centre.

The website is [www.radolca.si/en/]

Kranjska Gora

This is almost a perfect day trip for anyone including families. You can get to Kranjska Gora by bus (check timetables – I find a Google search is best). The bus journey (change at Lesce) can take up to two hours to get there. If you can drive it will only take 30 to 40 minutes; all the better. Having a car means you can tour around the area and visit places like the famous Russian Chapel which was built in 1917 by Russian prisoners of war in memory of the deceased during the construction of the Vršič Pass road.

In winter Kranjska Gora is a centre of snow sport activity, predominantly skiing, but even in the summer there are plenty of outdoor activities. This is a centre for cycling and hiking. For children (and adults) there is summer sledding, roller skating and Fairy-tale Land. These are just a few examples. There are extensive winter and summer activities for all ages and levels of fitness.

If you just want to mooch about and take it easy, there is a very pretty – and very small - Alpine old town.

Restaurants and coffee shops galore. The bright yellow Restaurant and Pizzeria Kotnik is a favourite. Café London at the Ramada hotel has an excellent apple strudel. An organised culinary journey once a week visits five eateries. Find out about that at the tourist information office.

If you are driving, with a bit of research you can plan your own tour. Although I am yet to try it, there is a glass topped tour bus giving 360 degree views. It connects places and attractions in the Upper Sava Valley.

The Tourist Information Centre in the town is at Kolodvorska ul. 1c 4280 Kranjska Gora Phone: +386 (0)4 580 94 40 e-mail: info@kranjska-gora.eu

The new website is very useful to help pick out the highlights [www.kranjska-gora.si/en]

Kranj, Škofja Loka and Tržič

In many ways, Kranj is an ordinary, busy small city, but there are several things to look out for on a visit. Start with Prešeren's House and Prešeren Grove. Prešeren is Slovenia's national poet. There are links to him in Bled, but this is where he lived and practiced.

See the Kokra River canyon just below the town and the bridges crossing it. There's the very beautiful and strange Plecnik's arcade and fountain. Near the Prešeren Museum you'll find Janez Puhar's house; Puhar was the inventor of glass photography. There is a labyrinth of tunnels under the town. For access to those as part of a guided tour contact Tourist Information: Glavni trg 2, 4000 Kranj Phone: +386 (0)4 238 04 50 e-mail: info@tourism-kranj.si

Other places to visit and spend time in include the beautiful Škofja Loka (http://www.visitskofjaloka.si/en)

with its old town, castle and grand houses and countryside to explore.

The small but intriguing Tržič; wander through its entries and pathways and find the museum which tells the story of shoe making in the region. Believe me, it is a lot more interesting than that sentence would suggest. Tržiški muzej, 4290 Tržič, Phone: +386 4 592 38 10.

If you are going by bus, there are two routes from Bled to Tržič. The route via Begunje na Gorenjskem and Slatna has great views south. Journey time is about 30 minutes by car, an hour by bus from Bled station. Check the route and bus times on Google Maps.

Some people try to compare Bled and Bohinj claiming one is better than another. It is neither a wise not fair comparison. Someone might prefer one over the other, but that is as far as it can go. They are different places with different offerings. Some activities are similar. I always think (right or wrong) that Bohinj is for the outdoor active person and Bled is mainly for the outdoor leisurely type. Why don't you do the comparison yourself? Bohinj is just about half an hour away by bus (Bohinj Jezero or Bohinj Zlatorog). The train goes to Bohinjska Bistrica (about an hour's walk to the lake in beautiful countryside).

Begunje na Gorenjskem is a favourite with an excellent restaurant and the Slavko Avsenik Museum. If you want to start collecting traditional Gorenjska costume or get a highly decorated and polished accordion, this is the place to visit.

Kropa is one of those places you are unlikely to visit, but actually you really should make the effort, particularly if you like decorative iron work (in which the town abounds) and social history that makes you glad you are living in the 21st century. Try to take the bus that offers you the free walking tour - although the visit to the museum will cost about €3. In previous years, Kropa was in the Hop On Hop Off bus route.

Insider knowledge - Ljubljana

Many people who come to Bled are visiting Ljubljana or basing themselves there. Visit Ljubljana has a marvellous website which has all the information you need for a visit. As there is so much to choose from let me provide one "insider tip". During the summer visit Ljubljana on a Friday for the Open Kitchen (Odprta kuhna). Ljubljana has many attractions. This is one of the best. Locals, tourists, office workers, passers-by enjoy the food from around the country and around the world, cooked in open-air kitchens for a fraction of the cost of a formal restaurant. And chefs and restaurateurs from Slovenia and beyond show off their best food. Dependent on weather.

The Hop On – Hop Off Bus

The service was an excellent way to get around the towns and villages nearby in 2015 and 2016. At time of writing, I understand that the bus will be touring the countryside again, but details are not yet available.

The bus has previously visited places which you might well miss otherwise. The Slovenian Alps and Gorenjska area are places of outstanding natural beauty which is one of the reasons so many tourists come to visit. But the popularity itself and the great numbers of visitors can cause terrible damage to the fragile natural environment. The intention of providing the buses is to help protect the environment by offering visitors and alternative to taking their own transport.

Check availability, routes and times at Tourist Information Centres in the area.

Serious hikers can start a walk away from Bled opening up new opportunities. Older people who are not quite as fit (like me) can see more of the country and find some great restaurants, forest walks, churches and all sorts of interesting places that you might not discover otherwise. It is well worth taking time for a trip to the Pokljuka plateau to visit the mountain pastures and traditional dairies.

A full day ticket will probably cost €5 and children under 10 travel free. More information can be found at Bled Turizm and Radol'ca Turizm and at the addresses below where you can pick up a time table.

TIC Bled, cesta Svobode 11, Bled. Phone: +386 (0)4 5741 122

TIC Radovljica, Linhartov trg 9, Radovljica Phone: + 386 4531 5112. info@radolca.si

Turizem Bohinj, Triglavska cesta 30, Bohinjska Bistrica Phone: +386 (0)4 574 75 90

Slovenia works hard to be a "green" country. Protecting the environment is a national objective. Ljubljana is a green capital of Europe. A fleet of cars traipsing around the roads beside the pastures of Gorenjska is not good for the environment. The bus helps.

I hope by this stage you are inspired to start your own research. You could do Bled in a day. I have lived there for over a year during two summers and one winter and visited many more times. I feel like I have only just begun to understand it.

PART 8 - A FEW WORDS OF SLOVENE

Slovene is not spoken by many more than the 2 million people who live in the country, and they do not expect foreigners to speak it. Consequently, very many Slovenes are multi-lingual. If you want to dabble in the language, most people, especially in shops, restaurants and bars, respond very warmly to anyone having a go. If you get it wrong, their English will be good enough to get you through any order or purchase.

English is used as a "bridge" language in many parts of Slovenia and throughout Bled. People from non-English speaking countries – Korea, Japan, China, Russia, even France and Spain – use English as a common language.

Italian and German are pretty widely spoken, too, especially further north in Kranjska Gora but it is always useful to have a few words of Slovene. A smile and "please/prosim", "thank you/hvala", "hello/dober dan", "good-bye/adijo" will get you a long way.

Greetings

When you go into a shop, a restaurant or a bar, you will be greeted with "Dober dan." everywhere. Literally it means "Good day", the response is "Dober dan" or just "Dan".

First thing in the morning you might walk into a hotel restaurant and be greeted with "Dobro jutro" ("Good morning") or late in the evening - after dusk - "Dober večer" (pronounced "ver-chair") "Good evening". "Good night" is "Lahko noč"

The "Hi" or "Hello" greeting is the less formal "živio". It is used among friends and especially by younger people.

So, "dober" is "good". In a restaurant, you are also going to hear "dober tek" which is "bon appetite" ... as we say in ... English.?.?

Please and thanks

"Prosim" is "please" and "hvala" is "thanks". Often in Bled you will hear people say "hvala lepa" which is the equivalent of "thank you very much". Although in other parts of Slovenia you might hear "Najlepša hvala" (pronounced "nai lepsha hwala").

Goodbyes and departures

The simple "adijo" ("aa - dee - o") is "'bye" but also used around Bled is the more formal "nasvidenje" – "goodbye". You will also hear "ciao". There are other "goodbye" words and phrases, but those will be enough to get you through a short visit.

Now you have enough to go into one of the Mercator shops in Bled, take something from the shelves, go to the checkout and say:

 "Dober dan" … Reply dober dan

 "Prosim" … And set down your purchases

As mentioned earlier, if you are buying loose fruit or vegetables, remember to weigh them before going to the checkout. Then hand over the money. The checkouts have a digital display of the bill so you don't need to learn the complicated numbers system ("devetnajst eurov in devetindevetdeset centov" is €19.99 … I think.)

"Rabim vrečko" if you need a bag. "To je vse" (toy-yo-say) "That is all" or "that is everything".

Exchange "Hvala" and "Hvala lepa". Then "Adjio" all round. You'll be just like a citizen of Bled. Well perhaps not. But it will raise a smile or two.

When you are buying something in a Mercator, the person on the checkout might ask you a question with the words "Pica" and "kartico" ("Imaš pica kartico?"). You are being asked if you have a Pica card, the Mercator loyalty card. Yes "da" and no "ne".

You will pay with Euro and cents or "kreditna kartica" "credit card".

More useful words

Airport	Letališče
Airplane	Letalo
Bus	Avtobus
Car	Avto
Car Hire	Najem avtomobile
Time-Table	Vozni red
Boat	Čoln
Boat hire	Najem čolnov
Train	Vlak
Train station	Železniška postaja
Entrance	Vhod
Exit	Izhod
Left	Levo
Right	Desno
I am [name]	Jaz sem [ime]
This is [name]	To je [ime]
Let's go for coffee	Gremo na kavo
Where are the shops?	Kje so trgovine?
Tomatoes	Paradižnik
Oranges	Pomaranče
Apples	Jabolka
Lettuce	Solata

Ice cream	Sladoled
Chocolate	Čokolada
Hot chocolate	Vroča čokolada
Mulled wine	Kuhano vino
Money	Denar
How much is that?	Koliko stane?
May I have the bill please?	Lahko dobim račun, prosim?

Appendix – General transport information and inside knowledge.

To Bled from Ljubljana Airport

Why, oh why is it so difficult for the independent traveller to get to Bled from the airport? And expensive, too? Yes, Bled may well be one of the principle tourist attractions in Slovenia, but getting to and from the airport is not attractive.

Here are some alternatives.

- **Call a friend.** If you are lucky enough to have friends in Bled, ask them for a lift. It will only be an hour out of their day.
- **Bus.** Awkward and time consuming but not expensive. You will need to take a bus to Kranj bus station. Buses leave on the hour (there are some service in between) and take about 20 minutes, then you will need to wait about 25 minutes for the Bled bus.
- **Taxi.** Likely to cost about €45. I use SMS [www.taxi-sms.si] phone or text +386 (0)70 999 699
- **Car Hire.** If I am with friends or family and can't cadge a lift with someone, I think that the most convenient way to get to Bled is to hire a EuropCar from the airport (always pre-book online) and return to the office in Bled. Same for the return journey. At just over €30 you will have the car for 24 hours and in that time, you can do some touring around the region. Go to Vintgar, Lake Bohinj, have an evening in Ljubljana. Other car hire companies probably provide the same pick up at airport return to Bled office service. Research online.
- Ales Zupancic of Zup Prevozi Transfers tells me he can offer 4 option of transfer (Economy, Economy flex, Business and VIP shuttle).

- o "Economy Shuttle: €13 per person (share ride door to door service). Departure from Airport at 11:15 or 16:45 Departure from Bled to Ljubljana Airport at 8:30 or 9:30 or 14:00
- o "Economy-Flex Shuttle (flexible shuttle): When you book your Economy-FLEX, you can OPT IN to share your transfer with another couple or solo traveller. There is no fixed timetable like our Economy shuttle. The timings of our shared transfers are flexible and are timed specifically around the flight arrival or flight departure times of our clients. Journey time is approximately 30 minutes. The driver will meet you at the airport arrivals with welcome sign.
- o "Business Shuttle: (private transfer). Departure after your flight. Flexibility, comfort and reliability at your convenience. Shuttle service between airport to any location in Bled. The driver will meet you at the airport arrivals with welcome sign.
- o "VIP-luxury Shuttle: Departure after your flight. Flexibility, comfort and reliability at your convenience. Shuttle service between airport to any location in Bled. The driver will meet you at the airport arrivals with welcome sign."

- Bus to Ljubljana: Leaves on the hour and takes about an hour to get to the bus and train station in Ljubljana. Should you be so moved, you could take the bus to Kranj then train to Ljubljana – takes longer and I can't think of one good reason to do that.

Airports

Ljubljana Brnik Airport (Letališče Brnik)

Web: www.lju-airport.si

Phone Passenger information: +386 4 20 61 981

E-mail: info@lju-airport.si

Maribor Airport

Web: www.maribor-airport.si

Phone: +386 (0)2 629 11 75

Email: info@maribor-airport.si

Bus Train and other Transport

The main bus station in Bled is very convenient to the centre of town and to the main hotel and hostel area. Bled is a minor hub and is limited in direct routes. Ljubljana - naturally - is the main hub, but Kranj, Lesce and Radovljica have important links.

Online Bus Time Table

There is what could best be described as a "quirky" timetable [www.ap-ljubljana.si/en/] For example

- It does not list Ljubljana Airport as a destination or departure. You need to know that the name to use is "Letališče Brnik"
- If you search for information from "Letališče Brnik" to "Bled", there is no result; "No matching connections for your request". That – presumably – is because the journey to Bled requires changing buses in Kranj. This shortcoming is a disappointment because the website was recently completely redesigned. Unfortunately, it is not tourist or visitor friendly. Best to use Google Maps (very useful, usually accurate), or find a person to ask in one of the bus stations.

Bus Operators

- Alpetour www.alpetour.si Phone +386 (0)4/20-13-210, promet@alpetour.si
- Arriva: www.arriva.si Phone 0907411 (in Slovenia)

Slovenian Railways (Slovenske železnice)

The timetable and price list for all trains in Slovenia can be found here [www.slo-zeleznice.si/en/passenger-transport/timetable]. Most journeys are worth taking just for the remarkable views and some amazing railway engineering.

There are two train stations: Bled Jezero above the lake on the northern shore. While fairly convenient to the camping site, it is about a 30 minute walk to the main centre. Lesce-Bled is about 4 km from Bled centre. There is a bus. Taxis between the two towns are expensive; up to 15 EUR for a 10-minute ride.

If you are really flash, there is a private airport in Lesce.

Bicycle Hire in Bled

There are lots of places to hire bikes and costs vary as do the types of bikes available. If you just want to scoot around town you should be able to pick up something inexpensive. For a more specialist model, try one of the adventure shops around the bus station.

Prices vary, even between outlets just a few paces apart. Spend a little time checking out your specific requirements. You could save yourself the price of several coffees and cakes later when you celebrate how active you have been.

Emergencies

Police emergency number 113 Ambulance emergency number 112

Bled Health Centre Mladinska cesta. 1 Tel. +386 4 575 40 00

Dental Clinic Prešernova cesta 15 +386 4 575 08 01 Opening Hours 9:00 am – 4:00 pm

Car trouble? Just a car problem or flat tire, call 1987 - AMZS (Auto-moto group, with technical centres all over Slovenia.). If you have a car crash, the police will give you the relevant information. If you have hired a car, you should have been provided with the emergency numbers by the hire company.

Public Transport Quick Links

The best thing to happen to travel information in this area is the arrival of Google Trips and the ease with which you can plot your journey on a Google Map. The bus and train networks can be (very) confusing for the first-time visitor. To get from A to C you might need to connect through B. Sometimes it is difficult to know where B is. But with Google maps you can more easily find your way.

ATM – Cashpoint - Bankomat

- Bankomat Gorenjska Banka: cesta Svobode 15, 4260 Bled (Near promenade and Spa Park)
- SKB Bank: Ljubljanska cesta 4, 4260 Bled. (Shopping Centre)
- NLB: Ljubljanska cesta 11, 4260 Bled. (Near Union bus stop)
- Bankomat GBKR: Ljubljanska cesta 30, 4260 Bled. (Petrol station on the left going into town)

Mobile Phones

You can buy a cheap mobile phone in the Tuš supermarket and from a vending machines beside the exit door at Ljubljana airport.

Wifi
Most of the cafés and restaurants have free wifi and there is free public wifi around the town centre.

About Davy Sims

Davy Sims first visited Bled in September 1996. He was working as a travel journalist with BBC reporting on Slovenia as a holiday destination. He returned several times and subsequently spent three extended periods in the town, living in Mlino, 200 metres from the lake in 2014, 2015 and 2016.

He has won broadcasting and new media awards in London, New York, Dublin and Belfast. He worked in BBC radio for most of his career, mainly in Radio Ulster but also in London as senior producer then chief producer in BBC Radio 1 and BBC Radio 4.

Davy began his career in 1978 aged 22 when he joined the local independent radio station for Northern Ireland, Downtown Radio. As a freelance he presented an evening weekday programme. He became fulltime a few months later.

At Downtown, Davy specialised in music and in particular new and emerging bands from Northern Ireland.

He joined the BBC in 1986 where he produced, magazine programmes, music programmes, news and current affairs, social action, travel, religious affairs and general programmes. In 1999 he became the first internet (BBC Online) producer in BBC Northern Ireland.

Davy now spends time between Northern Ireland and Slovenia. He occasionally lectures on Radio Production for Journalists in Dublin and on Journalism and Emerging Media in Ljubljana.

Davy can be found on Twitter @davysims, or through his blog davysims.com

Thanks

There are so many people to thank for their suggestions, ideas, inspiration and practical help. Mojca Polajnar has always been there to answer questions and help with suggestions. Tomaž Piber has been a great friend and enthusiastic supporter. But there are many more such as Lea Ferjan, Eva Štravs, Janez Fajfar, Tatjana Radovic. Also, Marija, Luka, Lili, Leo, Alen, Miha and Alenka. There are more.

A special thanks to Iain and Abbi Hay who proof read the book. I am very grateful and I look forward to seeing you in Bled before too long. And to my wife, Dawn for supporting me in these daft ideas.

Finally thanks to everyone one who sent feedback about the book to help me amend and improve the content.

End Piece

I have tried to ensure all the details in this book are correct as of 1 April 2017. Any significant changes will be included in subsequent versions or on the website www.firsthandguides.com

Always check with relevant websites and service providers including tourist information services before making any arrangements.

The book will be updated throughout 2017 as new events and stories emerge. If you have the Kindle Edition, you can receive the updates automatically on some models. Check with Kindle for information.

davysims.com

firsthandguides.com

https://www.amazon.co.uk/Davy-Sims/e/B01LWV138Q

Printed in Great Britain
by Amazon